The Power of Observation

Judy R. Jablon
Amy Laura Dombro
Margo L. Dichtelmiller

Foreword by Diane Trister Dodge

Washington, DC

Editor: Jean Bernard
Design by: Susan Cox-Smith
Illustrations by: Jennifer Barrett O'Connell
Production Coordinator: Chris Redwood

Published by:
Teaching Strategies, Inc.
P.O. Box 42243
Washington, DC 20015
www.TeachingStrategies.com

Publisher's Cataloging-in-Publication (*Provided by Quality Books, Inc.*)
Jablon, Judy R.
    The power of observation/Judy R. Jablon, Amy
Laura Dombro, Margo L. Dichtelmiller; foreword by
Diane Trister Dodge.—1st ed.
    p. cm.
    LCCN: 99-71241
    ISBN: 1-879537-36-2
    Includes bibliographical references.

    1. Observation (Educational method) 2. Child
development. 3. Teaching. I. Dombro, Amy
Laura. II. Dichtelmiller, Margo L. III. Title.

LB1027.28.J33 1999   371.3'9
                        QB199-997

Printed and bound in the United States of America

Third Printing: February, 2002

The *Power of Observation* is based on our experiences as caregivers and teachers and on the ideas and experiences of many educators with whom we have worked and to whom we owe tremendous appreciation.

A special thanks goes to Chayim Dimont, Marilyn Dolbeare-Mathews, Erlene Ellis, Amy-Beth Fischoff, Gail Gordon, and Barb Prevost, who worked with us intensively for a year providing observations of children they work with, answering our questions, and reflecting aloud about their personal experiences as observers. Their stories are the primary source of the examples and reflections included here.

Each of us has worked extensively with programs and individuals across the country whose questions, insights, challenges, and lessons learned about observing inspired us to write *The Power of Observation* and informed the ideas we chose to include. To the following individuals and programs we extend our appreciation: Lois Bell, Pam Prue, Judith Dighe, Carmen Van Zutphen, and Head Start and EEEP teachers and assistants from Montgomery County Public Schools in Maryland; the Early Learning Branch of the Maryland Department of Education and the teachers and assistants involved in the Maryland Model for School Readiness; Heather Charles and Traci Jones of Crystal Lakes Elementary School, West Palm Beach, Florida; the staff of Gamma House in Camden, New Jersey; Mary Cunningham-DeLuca, Brenda Davis, and Shelley Hawver of Community Action Agency Head Start and Early Head Start, Jackson, Michigan; Learning Readiness and Early Childhood Family Education programs, Minnesota; Betty Cook and the Minnesota Department of Children, Families, and Learning; Melissa Shamblott, Renie Willard, and Gail Roberts of the St. Paul Public Schools, Minnesota, and Jonathan Fribley, St. Cloud Public Schools, St. Cloud, Minnesota.

We extend appreciation to Samuel J. Meisels for his encouragement at the outset of this project. To Dorothea Marsden and Charlotte Stetson, special thanks for their willingness to read early drafts of the manuscript and get us on the right track. Thanks to Jim Levine, for answering our many questions and providing excellent advice and direction.

We thank everyone at Teaching Strategies for their confidence and support. Diane, your skill at clarifying ideas amazes us, and we thank you for the support you provided in shaping the final manuscript. Thanks to Larry Bram for coming up with our title and for getting *The Power of Observation* into the early childhood community. And to Jean Bernard, our editor; Susan Cox-Smith, our designer; and Jennifer Barrett O'Connell, our illustrator, thank you for contributions toward transforming our manuscript into a book.

We hope our book will show readers the close link among observing, building relationships with children and families, and effective caregiving and teaching.

Judy R. Jablon
Amy Laura Dombro
Margo L. Dichtelmiller
August 1999

This book greatly expanded my understanding of how powerful observing children can be. I believe it has the potential to truly transform the daily life and effectiveness of early childhood educators. And for us at Teaching Strategies, it represents a new emphasis in our work.

We decided to publish this book because we believe there is a strong link between effectively implementing a curriculum and observing young children. The authors—Judy, a co-author of *Building the Primary Grade Classroom: A Complete Guide to Teaching and Learning*; Amy, a co-author of *The Creative Curriculum for Infants & Toddlers*; and Margo, a colleague whose work on assessment we have admired and benefited from for many years—are especially qualified to provide the inspiration and guidance caregivers and teachers need to make this link. They bring to this task many years of experience working with young children and providing staff development on observation. As thoughtful educators, they listened respectfully to the stories of other teachers and caregivers and used what they learned to write this book.

All of us share a common goal: to enhance the quality of early childhood programs. While our focus at Teaching Strategies has been on developing curriculum resources, we know that support and training are essential if teachers are to understand and use a curriculum to guide their everyday decision making. Lately, we have been giving a great deal of thought to how we can help programs effectively implement the curriculum they are using. One of the key requirements is a good understanding of child development and in-depth knowledge of each child's unique abilities, interests, and needs. If we can help teachers, caregivers, and family child care providers to observe children systematically, they will have a wealth of information for implementing and individualizing curriculum and instruction.

The care and education of young children is important and challenging work. What makes this profession deeply satisfying and effective is the ability to form relationships with each child and family—not just the children who are easy to reach and the families that are eager to be partners. There are always children who seem to get lost in a group, whose behavior perplexes us, and whose strengths are not immediately obvious to us. And there are always families that resist our attempts to forge a partnership. We cannot afford to lose these children and families. We also owe it to ourselves to feel successful and satisfied rather than frustrated and ineffective in our work. That's where this book comes in.

As you set out to read *The Power of Observation*, I urge you to think of your own experiences working with young children. Which children get your attention each day? Which children mystify you? Think of a child you were not sure you could reach until you took the time to really get to know and appreciate that child's unique qualities. Knowing children as individuals—their interests, how they interpret experiences, how they learn best, their special skills and abilities—enables us to tailor our practices to help every child succeed.

Observation also helps build relationships with families. An experienced teacher and trainer, Elizabeth Servidio, once said to me, "It's very hard for parents not to like a teacher who really appreciates and likes their child." This book shows us how observation reveals what is unique and special about each child—even a child whose behavior challenges and frustrates us—and how this knowledge empowers us to reach families. It acknowledges the very real barriers to observing and offers a wealth of creative and practical strategies for addressing them. I am convinced that this book is a major contribution to the early childhood field, and to our efforts to support teachers and caregivers in implementing appropriate curriculum.

Diane Trister Dodge
President
Teaching Strategies, Inc.

CHAPTER 1

Introduction

The *Power of Observation* is a personal, reflective look at observing. In this book, we invite you to join us in exploring the vital connection between observing and your day-to-day work with children and families.

We define observation as watching to learn. Observing provides the information you need to build relationships with individual children and enable them to be successful learners. We learn about children by carefully watching them, listening to them, and studying their work. Watching and listening to children helps us understand what they are feeling, learning, and thinking.

Getting to know children as people and as learners gives you the information you need to be an effective decision maker in the classroom. With the information you learn from observing, you can select the right materials, plan appropriate activities, and ask questions that guide children in learning to understand the world around them.

Each child has a unique way of approaching learning. For example, one child may be an active explorer, intensely curious and imaginative. Another might be quiet, taking time to look around before getting involved in play or work. Every child is intrigued by something that ignites her wonder and provides insight into the essence of that child as a person and a learner. It may be music, frogs, penguins, painting, building with blocks, or something you can't yet imagine. As you watch, listen, and interact with children to discover their interests and approaches to learning, meaningful relationships develop.

The relationships that develop as you get to know and interact with children and family members affect everything that happens in your setting. When children and adults are recognized and respected, they feel good about themselves. When they feel a connection with you, they feel safe to explore, experiment, question, and test new limits—all prerequisites for learning. For all teachers, the key to effectiveness is trusting and responsive relationships. And observation is key to building these relationships.

A PERSONAL LOOK AT OBSERVATION

Like you, we have each worked with children and families and experienced our own successes and struggles with observing. In this book, we share our experiences and those of many other caregivers and teachers, inviting you to think with us about how observing already works for you, and about how to refine your observation skills and transform observing into an even more useful tool.

Here are some personal experiences that convinced us that observation and good teaching go hand-in-hand:

AMY: Johnny was a red-headed two-year-old who could empty a shelf of toys faster than any child I've ever known. I would spend the days he came to child care racing around after him, trying to keep some semblance of order. Around this time, I had to take a course on observing as part of my studies at Bank Street. I was upset. I knew how to watch children. I could see what they were doing. After about two months, it dawned on me: Observing wasn't just about what children do. It was watching them from the outside with the purpose of trying to understand what they are feeling and experiencing on the inside. This revelation helped me get to know Johnny. I began using observing to help me look at the world through his eyes and was surprised to see that he was bright, curious, and had a sense of humor. I noticed he loved music and would spend up to 5–10 minutes at a time strumming on a toy guitar. This was a far cry from my original opinion of him as chaotic. As I began sitting and singing with him and bringing out other instruments, something changed. I'm embarrassed to admit it, but one of those things was that I began liking him. He had to sense it because he started spending more time with me reading, talking, and preparing snack and less time scattering toys around. Our relationship, born out of observing, centered him and gave us the means to enjoy and learn from one another.

✧ ✧ ✧ ✧ ✧

MARGO: Tony, a four-year-old, came to my special education preschool with a great deal of advance notice. Many people on my classroom team had visited his home, a mobile home in a trailer park, and interviewed his parents, two very warm people who were mildly mentally retarded. My team members described Tony's somewhat unusual appearance: short for his age, large head, short arms, big glasses, and a very nasal voice. And they made long lists of objectives for Tony to work on in my classroom. When it was time for Tony to start school, I felt a little apprehensive because he had been described as "very active" at home. Based on all I had heard, I was expecting a child who struggled to learn and who would have a hard time adjusting to the order and routine of my classroom. Instead, I observed a very alert and curious child. True, he looked and sounded a little different. But as I watched him those first weeks of school, I realized he moved from one thing to another so quickly because everything was new to him. Although he was interested in other children and tried to approach them, he didn't know how to make friends. But Tony learned the rules and routines of the classroom within the first week. He began picking up on pre-academic skills almost immediately, and his language skills improved dramatically within the first two months. Although he had difficulty with gross and fine motor skills, they too improved with practice. As I look back, I marvel about how destructive it would have been if I had let my preconceived ideas about Tony influence how I saw him in my classroom. When I began to talk about his eagerness to learn and the rapid pace of his learning to my team members, they had a hard time believing it, but I kept encouraging them to come and watch him in the classroom.

✧   ✧   ✧   ✧   ✧

JUDY: It was my second year of teaching, and I struggled to find a way to connect with Rachel, a third grader in my classroom. But, no matter what I tried, we just didn't click. My observations of her continually reaffirmed my first impressions—she was unresponsive to activities, defying directions, and provoking her peers (and me). To be honest, I looked forward to the days she was absent. Mid-year, a student teacher, Lisa, came to work in my classroom. From the minute she arrived, I was aware of her competence with the children and what an asset she would be. The afternoon of her second day, the children were working in small groups on different projects related to our study of the Hopi. Lisa joined a group of children who were painting a mural of the desert. Rachel was in this group. Although I was busy with other groups, I periodically glanced over to see how Rachel's group was doing. At one point I noticed Rachel rush to the bookshelves to find a book with a picture of a cactus. Later I saw the group laughing together. After school I asked Lisa to tell me about her work with the group, but I said nothing about Rachel. Lisa had many observations about individual students. She commented on Rachel's enthusiasm and her sense of humor, but said nothing about her negativity. I told her about my experiences with Rachel. The next day I greeted Rachel by letting her know that Lisa had told me what a great sense of humor she had. Rachel smiled, said thanks, and rushed off to put her backpack away. All day I worked at seeing Rachel through Lisa's eyes, trying to set aside my feelings about her. I did notice many new things about Rachel that I just couldn't see before. In the first few days after Lisa came, Rachel and I had more positive interactions than we'd had all year. Lisa's arrival in my classroom had a big impact on me. I learned the value of seeking another perspective about a child when my own feelings were so strong.

In addition to our personal experiences as teachers, our experiences as staff developers confirmed to us the power of observation. As we work with teachers to improve their observation skills, or as they learn to use observational assessments, we find that some of them easily grasp how observing can help them and quickly incorporate it into their classroom routine. They constantly share how much more they know about their students. Others have more of a struggle. The teachers who struggle have pushed us to reflect more on our own experiences with observing and puzzle over how to make observing more accessible.

Gradually, as some of these teachers caught on, they began to interact with children in different ways, and became more excited about their work. We realized that too often teachers overfocus on the "how to" of observing. They get stuck trying to design the perfect record keeping system and worrying about whether they are doing it "right," and never get to the point when observing benefits their relationships and their work with children. Listening to the stories of teachers has helped us appreciate the role observing plays in supporting children's learning and eliciting effective caregiving and teaching.

BEYOND A SET OF SKILLS: OBSERVING AS AN ATTITUDE OF OPENNESS

If we all agree that observing is important, why is it so often a hit-or-miss affair and a source of great frustration? "I can go for months without giving observation a thought," one teacher told us. "I set out with good intentions," explains another. "Then at the end of the year, I find a pile of index cards in the drawer that I never looked at. It's frustrating."

We understand. We've been there. In the years since we left our teaching positions to develop educational materials and conduct staff development workshops, we have talked with hundreds of teachers with similar stories. Some of these conversations have occurred in one-on-one interviews, some during classroom visits, and others during workshops. A clear pattern has emerged: Teachers know observing is important. But most don't see themselves as effective observers and, thus, feel unable to reap the full benefits of observing.

Why does this gap exist? We believe the answer lies in how we have been taught to think about observing. Many of us were taught a set of skills, including looking at children's behavior, objectively recording what we see, and then analyzing our notes. Observing is all of these things, but it is so much more.

We believe that observing creates an attitude of openness and wonder that allows you to know and understand the children you work with every day. Observing is essential to building the trusting relationships with children and families that provide the foundation for a successful early childhood program. Only within the context of these trusting relationships can teachers promote children's development. Observing is so much more than a set of skills or another task to add to your already demanding schedule.

Getting to know a child is not a static process, though we each tend to form initial impressions—"She's quiet" or "He's trouble"—and often get stuck there. One teacher told us this about a quiet child, "I thought she was shy and hesitant until I began observing. Then I realized she was quiet, yes, but she was a leader and a risk-taker." Observing can help you go beyond your expectations or assumptions to see the many dimensions of a child that are revealed over time.

This subtle shift from seeing observing as a skill to seeing it as an open attitude essential to good teaching makes an enormous difference. Suddenly, observing is no longer something "out there" that you have to find time to do. Instead it becomes part of your everyday work. Watching, listening, reflecting, and relating are as important as anything else you do during the day, and this has implications for how you see your role as teacher.

For some, it is a jarring idea. "When I observe, I'm just standing there. But I'm a teacher. I'm supposed to teach," explained a first grade teacher at a recent observing workshop. "How am I supposed to do both?" he asked. Our answer: It isn't a question of either/or. Observing and good teaching are one.

For others, it takes time to adjust. A second grade teacher told us: "For me, observing regularly meant an attitude shift. But after I did it for awhile, it became part of who I am as a teacher."

 What are the implications of this shift for you?
How does it affect your sense of self as a teacher?
How does it affect your sense of self as an observer?

WHAT LIES AHEAD

There are many excellent books and videos available on observing children's learning that include information about child development and what to look for at different ages. This is not one of them. In *The Power of Observation*, we discuss the practice of observation and how to be a more effective observer. However, unlike other books about observing, our focus is on you, not the child.

Chapter 2 describes the power of observation as the way to get to know, respect, and appreciate children—the basis for building trusting, responsive relationships with them. These relationships are the foundation of effective caregiving and teaching.

In Chapter 3, we invite you to think about what you bring to your role as observer, and how you can use this self-awareness to be as objective as possible.

In Chapters 4 and 5, we turn to the practice of observing. In Chapter 4 you will find guidelines for effective observation. Chapter 5 takes a close look at the day-to-day decisions you make while observing and offers practical suggestions for observing in your setting.

Chapter 6 highlights how to use what you learn from observing to foster each child's competence and success, and as a result, to create and maintain a high-quality program for children and families.

Finally, in Chapter 7, we offer strategies for getting started and provide answers to frequently asked questions.

You may be a new caregiver or teacher or an experienced veteran. You may care for infants and toddlers or teach third graders. You may work in a child care center, family child care home, preschool, Head Start program, or school. Regardless of the setting or the age group you teach, you—and all the other early childhood teachers we know—care deeply about children and want to do a good job. Every day you work hard to help children and their family members feel connected and competent. You promote their learning by offering an environment and experiences that invite them to explore, discover, and construct meaning. It isn't always easy, and yet you persevere.

Observing can play an important role. The more you observe, the better you will know children and how to promote their success as learners. Their success, in turn, will help you feel successful, and the cycle will continue. Your challenge is to take full advantage of the wealth of insights observing offers you day in and day out. *The Power of Observation* can help.

CHAPTER 2

Using Observation to Build Relationships

When you observe, you slow down, listen to a child more carefully, and pause to reflect before stepping in to offer some direction or a helping hand. You see and respond to who a child is and what a child needs. Observing helps you build relationships by revealing the uniqueness of every child—including the child's temperament, strengths, personality, work style, and preferred mode of expression.

For example, when you observe that Shawna is an infant who gets upset when things change, you may respond by keeping her daily routine as consistent as possible. Because you know that Tommy naturally moves toward the painting table at choice time and creates vivid, detailed pictures of places you visit on class trips, you might observe him at work to see what he found interesting at the bakery so that you can suggest he write about it later. Observing that typically quiet Alice is an incredible builder might lead you to invite her, first privately, then publicly, to describe one of her block structures to the other children during group time.

Here is what some caregivers and teachers have to say about how observing has influenced their way of being with children and their relationships with them:

It is the act of observing—of giving someone my attention and trying to understand that child—that opens my heart. As I observe, I begin to get to know a child. A feeling bridge is built. The details I observe start to come together, and I begin to see what the child needs from me.

✿   ✿   ✿   ✿   ✿

Observing slows me down. I listen to children more. I engage with them instead of teaching at them.

✿   ✿   ✿   ✿   ✿

I use observation to get to know children better—to figure out how to relate to them better and to teach them better. By observing, I know that Thalia has a sense of humor because I have seen that little smile and the twinkle in her eye. I'm going to figure out ways to get that twinkle in her eye a little more often.

 Reflect on a child you know well. How would you describe your relationship with the child? How did your relationship begin? What made you start feeling connected to the child? How did it feel? What role did observing play?

Observing fosters your relationships with children by helping you:

✿ get to know children,

✿ respect and appreciate children, and

✿ intervene in ways that enable children to be successful learners.

GETTING TO KNOW EACH CHILD

Think about the children you work with each day. Write down each child's name. Next to each name write down the child's age and something you have observed about that child.

Here are some children we know and what we wrote when we did this exercise:

Alex (6 mos):	Babbles back when I talk with him
Maria (26 mos):	Cries a lot lately when her grandmother leaves in the morning
Tony (3 yrs):	Sits and watches every morning before joining in
Baili (3 yrs):	Told me about making dumplings with her parents over the weekend
Katy (5 yrs):	Drew a picture of Iris, her cat
William (5 yrs):	Built a barn with stalls and a milking machine
Denise (7 yrs):	Counted out coins for another child's change at our classroom bookstore
Alexander (7 yrs):	Reading his third book about whales

Now it's your turn. On a sheet of paper, list your observations.

 How did it go? Were you surprised to find that you couldn't think of something to write about some children? Did you forget to put some children on your list, children who have been invisible to you?

You most likely found that you know some children better than others. Most teachers do. Who are these children? Teachers we have talked with say they know most about the children they feel connected to in some way. These are usually children whose personalities, behavior, and/or family's values strike a familiar chord in the teacher. Teachers also seem to know something about those children who by themselves or with family members create a big presence. Ironically, sometimes the unique personalities, strengths, and needs of these children are blurred by teachers' own experiences, assumptions, and prejudices. We'll talk more about this in the next chapter.

There is always something new to learn about a child—even a child you think you know well. Try to make a habit of asking questions (or acknowledging your questions). This will help you get to know a child and keep track of who that child is becoming over time.

Questions to Help You Get to Know Children

What are some of your questions about the children with whom you work? Observing can help you learn about a child's:

○ **Health and physical development.** How would you generally describe the child's health? What do the child's health records reveal? Have family members raised any questions or concerns about a child's health or development? Have any occurred to you?

○ **Temperament.**[1] Can a child generally be described as flexible? Slow-to-warm or fearful? Feisty or intense? Though children don't fall into neat categories, having a sense of a child's temperament may help you to predict and understand that child's behavior.

---

[1] Infant researchers Alexander Thomas and Stella Chess have identified three basic types of temperaments. The program for Infant/Toddler Caregivers, developed by West/Ed Far West Laboratory for Educational Research and Development in collaboration with the California Department of Education, has named these flexible, fearful, and feisty.

○ **Skills and abilities.** What does the child do well? What does the child find challenging? What skills is the child currently working on?

○ **Interests.** What topics cause a child's eyes to light up? What does the child talk about? What does the child do when given the opportunity to choose?

○ **Culture and home life.** What do you know about the child's culture and life at home? For example: Who are the members of the child's family? What language is spoken in the child's home? Do family members play different roles in child rearing? How do family members interact with one another? How is discipline handled?

○ **Approach to learning.** How does the child approach new material? How does the child interact with materials? What is the child's preferred way of expressing himself or herself?

○ **Use of verbal language.** Does the child speak? If so, how much language does he or she have? With whom does the child talk? Other children? Other adults? What kinds of things does the child talk about? Is the child comfortable speaking one-on-one? In a large group?

○ **Use of body language.** How does the child move? Does the child use gestures? Is the child physically expressive?

○ **Social interactions with adults and peers.** Does the child interact with others? Does the child seem comfortable interacting with adults? Other children? Familiar people? New people? How does the child initiate interactions? What kinds of activities does the child do with others? How does the child handle conflicts with others? In what situations does the child seek adult help?

Observing to Find Answers

Specific questions give you a focus for your observations and help you find answers. Over time, you have repeated opportunities to witness children practicing skills, demonstrating knowledge, and exhibiting behaviors in a familiar and comfortable environment. You can observe not only what children know, but also how they think and solve problems. By collecting observations over time, you find the answers to your questions and build a picture of children's performance and progress without interfering in any way with their daily activities or "natural" behavior.

For example, when Laura, an infant caregiver, senses something amiss with five-month-old Kara's fine motor development, she goes to the observational checklist she uses regularly to monitor children's fine and gross motor development. Based on her observations, she realizes Kara isn't bringing both hands to midline, while Taylor, who is the same age, does so frequently. Laura plans to continue observing. She will talk to the physical therapist who consults with the program about ways to help Kara reach this milestone.

Kathy's teacher photographed the castle she constructed in the block area. Another day, he quickly sketched the pattern block design Kathy, age 4, made in the math center. On yet a third occasion, he saved a collage Kathy made. When it comes time to evaluate Kathy's performance and progress, his judgments about her sense of balance and symmetry will be based on these and many other observations.

A third grade teacher monitors Brendon's developing spelling skills by observing him as he writes and studying his written work. Here are the brief notes she recorded at three different times.

3/12:	Conference w/me, B self-corrected 3 words.
3/24:	Taking more chances writing "hard words" (Atlatik Osen—Atlantic Ocean).
4/20:	Using word cards to help w/science writing.

These collected observations enable her to evaluate Brendon's spelling. They provide specific examples of Brendon's behavior and accomplishments to share with his parents at their upcoming conference. And they provide data she needs to determine how to intervene in ways that help Brendon continue to see himself as a successful learner.

Getting to know children by asking questions and assessing their learning is one step in building a relationship, but there are more. Engaging in a relationship with children also involves finding something you respect and appreciate about each child—something that draws you in and makes you invested in that child's well-being and success.

RESPECTING AND APPRECIATING CHILDREN

Think about a friend who accepts you as you are and takes pleasure in your accomplishments. How do you feel when you are with this person? At ease? Competent? Confident? Acknowledged for who you are? Trusting? Proud? Supported? Secure? Willing to take risks?

These feelings are the building blocks of self-confidence that we want all children to experience. How the children in your group feel about themselves depends in large part on how you respond to their actions, ideas, questions, and work. And how they feel about themselves, in turn, will influence how they feel about and interact with others. As children come to see that you respect their work, their discoveries, and their ideas, they will come to respect themselves.

Sometimes your respect and appreciation for children blossoms as your picture of them becomes clearer. Often, this also strengthens your relationship. You can convey your respect and appreciation to children in many ways; here are just a few:

○ Listen and respond to what children tell you through their sounds, facial expressions, gestures, words, and body language.

- Show children you care about what they do and say by commenting on what you see them doing, then pausing and waiting for their response (e.g., saying, "Your building is really tall," then pausing for a response, or after watching for several minutes commenting, "I notice that when you poured water through the top of the water wheel, the wheel began turning around").

- Ask open-ended questions that invite many responses and let them know that there is no right or wrong answer (e.g., What do you think might happen next in the story? What do you remember about our trip to the fire station? Why do you think Clifford did that?).

- Demonstrate your recognition of children's competence by providing opportunities for them to help and teach one another. And don't hesitate to ask children a question or for some help.

- Show children that you have time to listen and be with them. Sit down with a child instead of talking on the run. Don't let interruptions by other children distract your time with a child. Explain that you are busy and will see them when you are finished.

There will be instances, of course, when a child pushes one of your buttons or rubs you the wrong way. It can be uncomfortable to admit you have negative feelings about a child, and all too often teachers tend to keep them a secret. If you acknowledge these feelings to yourself and/or a trusted colleague, it will help you get a handle on them and avoid letting them color your daily interactions. How you respond to children shapes how children see themselves and interact with others. Thus, how you feel about them is as important as what you say or do together.

The Powerful Influence of Your Feelings about Children

Children have an uncanny ability to tune into how you feel about them. They sense your feelings in the way you hold them, the expression on your face, and your tone of voice.

Because you play such an important role in their lives, they care about how you feel and they want your approval. Like the ripples caused when you throw a stone into a pond, your feelings about individual children have a far-reaching influence that touches children's developing sense of self, their impressions of and interactions with one another, and even how their parents view you and them. Here is what three teachers have observed about the impact of their feelings:

> Christiane cried inconsolably after her mother left in the morning. Her crying was so intense it frightened me. I would hold her, hoping the crying would stop—but it didn't. One day I realized it was all right that she was upset and that I could help her. I held her as usual, the only difference being my sense of confidence that she would be OK. She cried as usual, but by the next day, her sobs began turning to sniffles after only a few minutes. It's amazing—the power of your feelings—isn't it?

☼　　☼　　☼　　☼　　☼

> As I build relationships with kids, they know I am interested in them. They relax with me, and I'm more relaxed too. They tell me wonderful stories and jokes. We laugh a lot. When the room is more relaxed, I'm more willing to set up cooperative active learning experiences that the kids enjoy and learn from.

☼　　☼　　☼　　☼　　☼

> When Sarah first came into my class, I tiptoed around her—and her mother. They both had a reputation for being difficult, and I wanted to avoid a scene. I recently told Sarah's mom, "I really like your daughter." She cried because no one had ever said that to her before. I told her that her daughter is a good

worker and cooperates with other children. Funny thing is, at first, I had assumed Sarah was a problem, and I used to jump to the conclusion that when there was a dispute among a group, she was the cause. Observing helped me see her for who she is and appreciate her—and helped me forge an alliance with her mom.

But what about those children—and there are always some—whom you find unappealing or annoying and, to be honest, shy away from? We know you want to give your best to all children—but some children require more effort than others. The first step is to look beyond a child's drooling, crying, constant activity, shyness, troublemaking, or whatever other aspect of behavior you find off-putting. The next step is to find a point of connection.

CONNECTING WITH CHILDREN

Remember Amy's story about Johnny? Her discomfort in dealing with this active toddler could have made her constantly restrict his behavior. Put yourself in Johnny's place for a moment. How would this have made you feel about yourself? Instead, through observing, Amy came to see him as a unique individual and to appreciate his zest for life and sense of humor. This doesn't mean she never said no or set limits on his behavior. But her interactions were colored by her respect and newfound delight in him. As a result, Johnny was helped to feel good about himself as an explorer rather than seeing himself as someone thwarted at every turn.

Do you have a Johnny in your group? Can you use observation to find a point of entry into a relationship with this child by asking yourself such questions as:

* ✿ What issues is the child dealing with?

* ✿ In what situations does the child seem most comfortable?

* ✿ What causes the child's eyes to brighten, what brings a smile?

- ✿ What does the child do well?

- ✿ What does the child talk, read, or write about?

- ✿ What does the child paint, build, or draw?

- ✿ What are the main themes of the child's dramatic play?

- ✿ Is there an adult, child, or activity that seems to draw the child out?

Sometimes the answers are evident—once you take the time to stop and look. When you observe that Carlos talks constantly about his new baby brother and spends all his time in dramatic play wanting to be a baby, you have a clue about how to approach him and insight into why he's been so clingy and whiny lately. Discovering during recess that Ralene, so annoying during group time, is a terrific climber and that she runs with great coordination and enthusiasm leads you to tell her that you have noticed her wonderful outdoor skills. Her pleasure in your validation results in several positive interactions, and you begin to see her in a new light. Although her behavior at group time may not look different, you feel differently about it. Your change in attitude toward her may have a positive influence on her. Or you may incorporate her observed strength into a group time conversation. Asking children to describe their favorite things to do outside might provide Ralene with a way to make a meaningful contribution and give her a positive experience during a routine that is typically hard for her. Her feeling of success in this situation is likely to lead to other successes.

Sometimes answers are not as apparent. Indeed, you may not even know where to begin looking. You realize you do not know enough, so you go back to the beginning—getting to know a child.

Other times discovering a point of contact with a child may require some flexibility and openness on your part. Getting to know the child who delights in the frogs she discovers during a class trip to a nearby pond may mean that you have to move beyond your negative attitude toward amphibians. When you learn that a child you assumed to be a natural "trouble-maker" knows a lot about the space shuttle program, your plans for creating a store in the dramatic play area may end up being set aside—at least temporarily—to make room for a refrigerator-box space capsule and mission control center.

FOSTERING CHILDREN'S COMPETENCE AND SUCCESS

Observing gives you the information you need to make decisions about when and how to intervene with children. You want your actions to help children see themselves as successful learners and, at the same time, strengthen your relationships with them. You can use the information you learn from observing to create your classroom's physical and social environment and to plan your daily routines and activities. The environment you create leads children to certain kinds of discoveries, thinking, and the acquisition of certain skills. Your role is to facilitate children's thinking and learning as they discover their own meaning of their experiences.

Too often, however, teachers intervene in ways that are oriented toward an activity, not toward children and their learning. Think, for example, about the infant teacher who takes babies' hands in hers to glue cut-out umbrellas to a collage for her "Spring Showers" bulletin board. Or the second grade teacher who brings out the unifix cubes and persists in conducting a lesson on fractions when children clearly are fascinated by creating symmetrical patterns. Interventions such as these lead to frustration instead of learning.

As you get to know children, and your respect and appreciation for them grows, your decisions about how and when to intervene will more likely be based on children's interests and needs. This is the essence of individualizing.

Ask yourself three basic questions before intervening:

✧ Should I step back and give children the space and time they need to make a discovery or solve a problem independently?

✧ Does the child need me to step in and help?

✧ If I step in, what should I say or do?

Sometimes the best thing you can do to support a child's learning is to step back and let the child experience something. Taking a few moments to observe a child at play or work may be just what you need to figure out if you should stay out of the action. When you do step in, rely on your observations to ask the right questions to stimulate and stretch the child's thinking.

Often you don't have to say much. A simple comment or question, such as, "Tell me how you decided to use the colors on your painting that way" or "I noticed that you seem to be putting the unifix cubes in a special order. Do you have a rule?" can do the trick. Our colleague Diane Trister Dodge tells a great story about a four-year-old who was sorting a group of objects. The child put a pig and a cup in the same group. At first, his teacher started to intervene. But then she asked, "Tell me about your plan for sorting. How did you decide what things to put in the same group?" The little boy responded, "Well, I'm not really sure if a pig gives milk, but if it does, it needs a cup to put it in."

Here are some examples of how observing can help you decide what to do:

Step in and make a suggestion

You notice that each time a child sets a square block on top of the cylinder the blocks topple. You could help or you could wait to see what happens. Watching lets you learn about the child's problem-solving skills. If after awhile, you sense she is frustrated, you might step in and comment, "I see that you have tried putting the square on the top of the cylinder and it keeps toppling. Why do you think that is happening?" Then wait and see what she says or does. She may have only needed you to describe what she was doing to come up with another idea. Or, she may need you to suggest that she try putting a larger block on the bottom. If that works, you may ask, "Why do you think it is not falling over?" By giving her time to experiment and then being there to offer support when she needs it, you have encouraged her to use trial and error—a basic problem-solving strategy—and provided her with helpful language—cylinder, square, balance, top, bottom—for thinking about the problem.

Wait and watch

Imagine you have just come back from a walk and you notice an infant is trying to pull off his hat. Should you step back or take action? You observe and see that he looks engaged and determined as he pulls on it. You decide to step back and keep your eye on him. Two minutes later, he is smiling, the hat in hand. If he had started getting upset or frustrated, if the hat got stuck and was covering his eyes or nose, you would have intervened in a different way.

Describe a child's actions

You see a preschool child who is struggling to fit Legos together. You wait and watch. She tries several different pieces and finally comes up with a solution. She cries out, "Finally!" You respond with, "I noticed you tried many different pieces until you got one to fit. That was good work."

Use prior knowledge to prevent a conflict

Imagine two first graders struggling over one bottle of glue. What you know from prior observation will help you decide what to do. Because one child has been hitting lately, you might step in and offer a cup of glue with two popsicle sticks, a second bottle of glue, or simply hand the glue bottle to one child and say to the other, "I know it is hard to wait but it will be your turn in a minute." By intervening, you aid both children, and the child who has been hitting learns how it feels to resolve a conflict without hurting another child.

Use observations to foster competence and success

Think back to the children we talked about at the beginning of this chapter. In the chart that follows, you'll see decisions we might make to promote their learning based on our knowledge, appreciation, and respect for them. The next time you observe, think about how something you see influences how you intervene to support a child's success.

CHILD'S NAME/AGE	WHAT WE OBSERVED	WHAT WE MIGHT DO
Alex (6 mos)	Babbles back when you talk with him	✧ Promote his language development by talking about what you are doing as you feed, change, and dress him. Give him time to respond with sounds and gestures.
Maria (22 mos)	Cries lately when her grandmother leaves in the morning	✧ Be available to support her when it is time for grandmother to say good-bye. ✧ Show respect and let her know she can share her feelings with you by listening to her and acknowledging her feelings. ✧ Show her the picture of her family hanging on the wall.
Tony (3 yrs)	Sits and watches every morning before joining in	✧ Greet and welcome him when he arrives. Explain what is going on in the room. Give him the time he needs to survey the scene and feel comfortable.
Baili (3 yrs)	Told about making dumplings with her parents over the weekend	✧ Provide cultural continuity by talking about foods children eat at home. ✧ Add books with pictures of foods from different cultures to the library corner. ✧ Invite Baili's parent(s) to come prepare dumplings or another favorite dish with the children.

CHILD'S NAME/AGE	WHAT WE OBSERVED	WHAT WE MIGHT DO
Katy (5 yrs)	Drew a picture of her cat, Iris	✿ Help Katy bridge her worlds of home and kindergarten by asking about Iris when you discover a picture of a cat in the book you are reading together.
William (5 yrs)	Built a barn complete with stalls and a milking machine in the block area	✿ Ask him to talk about how he helps his older brother milk the cows in the barn. ✿ Reinforce what he already knows by hanging up pictures of the interior and exterior of barns in the block area.
Denise (7 yrs)	Counted out coins for another child's change at the classroom book-store	✿ Encourage this new skill by inviting her to help another child count change when it is his turn to be the cashier.
Alexander (7 yrs)	Reading his third book about whales	✿ Build on his interest by suggesting he look for other books and perhaps videos about whales—and maybe other marine mammals—during our next visit to the library. ✿ Invite him to share what he has learned during group time.

We encourage you to step back occasionally and enjoy the children you work with. Everyone will benefit. Your work will be so much more satisfying, your relationships with parents enriched by the stories you share with them, and the children will thrive and blossom.

When you observe, you slow down, listen to a child more carefully, and pause to reflect on who a child is and what a child needs. Observing can help you build relationships by helping you:

- ☼ **Get to know the children**. There is always something new to learn about a child. Make a habit of asking questions and observing to find answers to help you get to know a child and keep track of that child's development.

- ☼ **Respect and appreciate children**. Children have an uncanny ability to tune into your feelings about them. Observing can help you find a point of entry to enable you to connect with a child.

- ☼ **Foster children's competence and success**. When you observe you get information that can help you decide how and when to intervene in ways that enable children to experience themselves as successful learners.

We have been talking about building relationships. In the next chapter, we turn our attention to you—the observer and relationship-builder.

CHAPTER 3

You as Observer

An observation is like a photograph—it captures a moment in time. As an observer, you are like the photographer, focusing on some things, ignoring others. Also, like the photographer, you bring yourself—your ideas, preferences, and perceptions—to the act of observing.

We can never eliminate the personal side of observing, nor would we want to. But we do need to be aware of it because what you bring to observing shapes how you see children and families, which in turn affects your relationships with them.

Have you ever observed a child's behavior and thought, I've seen this a hundred times? Then, before you know it, you find yourself forming an assumption based on one observation: "This child is aggressive" or "This child is shy."

For most of us, the moment we make an assumption, images come to mind of previous experiences or events that relate to the assumption. Imagine a computer in the back of your head and, just as you make an assumption, the computer's screen shows a script describing how to act. You begin interacting with a child according to this script, which influences how the child responds. The first round of a continuing cycle has begun. The potential for getting to know, respect, and appreciate a child for who he or she is gets lost and, with it, the opportunity to support the child's learning in the best way possible.

Why does this happen? Often it happens simply because knowing something is far more comfortable for most of us than not knowing. The more quickly we can get a handle on individual children, the more competent and in control we feel. In addition, people working with young children are often juggling many balls at the same time and have an enormous number of demands on their time. As a result, they tend to do things in a hurry—including forming hasty opinions of children. Let's face it, making snap judgments is human nature. But if we understand this tendency, we can take steps to guard against it.

In this chapter, we invite you to think about what you bring to observing and the steps you can take to make sure that your pictures of children and relationships with them reflect who they actually are rather than who you assume they are.

WHAT YOU BRING TO OBSERVING

Your culture, your individual temperament, interests, feelings, and your professional knowledge and experience color the lens through which you observe. When you are aware of these factors you increase the chances that your observations will give you insight into children, and that your relationships with them will be authentic. Over time you will learn to trust your observations and come to depend on what you bring to help you tune into a child's uniqueness. An infant/toddler teacher describes what this is like for her:

> Observing is about understanding human beings. That's something I try to do in my everyday life. I peer into people and try to get to know them. At work, I may have trouble remembering what a child's coat looks like or whose spoon is whose. But when it comes to a child's temperament and personality, I see things clearly. It is why I went into this work in the first place.

You will also come to recognize those instances when your perspective may interfere with seeing clearly. Consider this experience of a first grade teacher:

> Travis is one of those kids who is always tapping you on the leg to get your attention. The fact that he is always right there next to me annoys me—maybe it's something about my need for independence. Anyway, I recently found myself in the position of having this kid literally right by my side and realizing I don't know much about him. I'm trying to take a deep breath, accept that he is sticking close because he needs support, and observe to try to get a clearer picture of what is going on with him.

 What do you bring to observing that helps you tune into the special qualities of each child and build a responsive relationship? What else do you bring that keeps you at a distance and gets in the way of building a relationship?

Your Culture

Each of us has a set of beliefs about ourselves, as well as attitudes, assumptions, and expectations about people and events around us—some that we may not even be aware of. This is culture; it is what makes each of us who we are. Anthropologist Ward Goodenough defines culture as "a set of standards or rules for perceiving, believing, acting, and evaluating others."[2]

Our culture is reflected in our communication, expectations, and, therefore, our observations of others. How close you stand when you talk with someone, when you pause for the other person to respond, or if you meet someone's gaze when a person looks at you are examples of behaviors determined by culture. Too often when we think about culture what comes to mind is

---

[2] W. Goodenough, *Culture, Language, Society,* Menlo Park, CA: Benjamin Cummings Publishing, 1981.

how holidays are celebrated, what people wear, or the food they eat. But culture is much more than holidays, dress, and food and is much more subtle.

Indeed, it is so subtle that it influences how we expect people to behave and how we interpret their behavior. When people behave differently from what we expect or when we misinterpret their behavior, we may feel confused, frightened, or even look at them negatively. These feelings get in the way of seeing, getting to know, and relating to a person.

Here are some examples of how cultural differences—or conflicting beliefs—got in the way of teachers as they worked to build relationships with children and families.

Beliefs about child rearing

Chloe's toddler son, Georges, sleeps with his parents just as Chloe did when she was a child. Rebecca, Georges's favorite teacher at child care, knows this and cannot accept it. She is constantly hinting that Georges should be sleeping in his own crib. Chloe no longer feels comfortable talking with her. As a result, Rebecca, who spends eight hours a day, five days a week with Georges, is missing out on the opportunity to learn more about Georges's life at home and cannot offer Georges the degree of continuity between home and child care that she could if she and Chloe were working together as partners.

Beliefs about appropriate ways to communicate

At home, dinnertime was filled with busy, interactive conversation during which Isabella's grandmother, mother, father, and sisters all talked continuously, adding to each other's stories as if they were weaving a quilt together. Often several family members talked at once—no one ever thought that adding on to someone's story was an interruption. Isabella came to her preschool classroom eager to share her ideas and experiences and add to the stories of others, just as she does every day at home. However, each time Isabella spoke, her teacher hushed her, saying that she had to raise her hand to talk. At first, Isabella would speak up while simultaneously raising her hand, but this led to more hushing. After awhile, Isabella stopped talking. In this case of cultural differences, everyone ended up losing. Isabella's enthusiasm about school and her sense of herself as a joyful contributor was diminished. Her teacher's need for order prevented her from connecting with Isabella and teaching her how to be an effective group member at school.

Beliefs about children's independence
To Claudia, Rami's behavior was annoying. He worked extremely slowly, demanded her attention, and would not complete tasks independently. Rami and Claudia spent much of his third grade year working against each other—she pushed him to move faster and with more independence and he responded by moving even slower and needing more attention. Although Claudia had a vague sense that Rami's behaviors related to his home life and cultural background, her irritation with him interfered with her willingness to gain support from Rami's mother. On the few occasions when Claudia expressed her frustration about Rami, his mother tried to offer insights. Among other things, she told Claudia that, as the only son, and the youngest child in the family, Rami was not expected to do things on his own. Because of Claudia's frustration and irritation, she wasn't able to hear these explanations, so Rami continued to be a challenge.

Going beyond cultural differences
Like the teachers in these stories, it is easy to assume that your way is the right way. We all do this sometimes. The danger is that it closes you off to seeing other possibilities. When it comes to culture, there are many right ways.

Understanding culture and cultural differences is not easy, even when you have the best intentions and you and the children's families are both invested in the children's well-being and learning.

Here are some strategies that can help you get beyond cultural differences and build trusting relationships:

✿ Be aware of how your culture—your attitudes, beliefs, and expectations—shapes you as a person and teacher. This will give you some insight into the deep influence culture has on others, including the children and families with whom you work.

✿ Observe to discover similarities and differences between your culture and those of children and families. Like most of us, you may find similarities easier to deal with than differences. But remember, differences exist and we have to recognize them before we can bridge them. Be open and try to accept and acknowledge both.

✿ Find out more about what culture means to each family and the ways in which it is reflected in the family's behavior. Continue to observe, listen, and, as trust grows, share some of your questions and your own experiences and beliefs.

Cultural collisions and tensions between teachers and family members are a part of life. If parents of the same child disagree, for example, about the right way to respond to a child's challenging behavior based on how they were raised, it is no surprise that teachers and parents such as Claudia and Rami's mother are caught short by differences, not only between their own cultures, but between the cultures of home and child care or school. The challenge is to get beyond asking what is right and wrong in order to see another person's point of view and communicate openly, always keeping in mind your common goal of supporting the child.

Your Individuality

What and how you see is shaped by who you are. This partially explains how two people can observe the same child and see different things. Through the following stories we explore how different personal characteristics can influence observation.

Temperament
One teacher described how differences in temperament affected how she and the child's parent experienced the child.

> It was early in the year and I was having a conference with Laura's mom. I was ready to share how well I thought Laura was doing in first grade. She had begun to read, she did her work quietly and independently—overall I was really pleased with how she was doing. Her mom began the conference expressing concerns about Laura's shyness. She said that Laura didn't talk much at home—she didn't play with other kids in the neighborhood. Basically, she said that Laura was really different from her older sister and even herself. They were both bubbly—always talking and getting into everything. I thought about this a lot after the conference. I guess you could say I'm a pretty quiet person. I connected with that in Laura. But during the conference—well, it was like we were seeing two different children.

In addition to illustrating how people's perceptions of the same child can be different, the story about Laura describes how much more easily you can connect with a child when the child's way of being in the world matches yours. But what happens when there isn't a match? It can be much harder to observe and appreciate children who are different from you, as you will see from this family child care provider's story.

> Simon is a really active toddler. His idea of a good time is taking two cars and crashing them together. He loves the noise and really gets into it. I can't stand it. As soon as I see him

getting the cars from the shelf, I jump in and suggest he try something else.

Someone else observing him might enjoy Simon's enthusiasm and, rather than attempting to change his behavior, might extend his play by showing him how to make a road with long blocks.

Interests

Have you ever gone to a movie with someone and then, when it is over, realize that each of you tuned in to different parts? Perhaps you focused on the characters while your friend was fascinated by the cinematography. Some of us notice the physical aspects of people or things—how people, objects, or places look. Some notice motion and action, others tune into sound or emotions.

Your interests and preferences significantly influence how you see and experience children and how you shape and observe the classroom environment, as illustrated by this teacher's story.

> I like lots of activity. When I first started teaching, my classroom was kind of like my home. There were always new projects going on, lots of conversation, and music was often playing. One day, a more experienced teacher commented that things looked a little chaotic as opposed to busy. I had never noticed. But when I stepped back, I could see that he was right. There is still lots going on, but I've learned over the years to observe to see how much activity is the right amount for the children in my group.

Feelings

We encourage you to trust your feelings as an observer. If you feel edgy or a little uncomfortable as you observe a child, it probably means something. Ask more questions, look a little more, and see if you can identify your own feelings, find a way to make a connection, and begin forming a relationship with the child.

Here are two examples of teachers recognizing their own negative feelings about children and using observation to find other ways to look at a child.

There are times I can't see beyond the negative about a child. Sometimes I know what's bugging me. For example, last year there was a girl in my room who loudly demanded my attention. She was hard for me to deal with at first. I could hear my parents telling me, "Ask politely," and at the same time I was a little envious of her boldness. Once I realized this about myself, I could turn my attention to getting to know her. Other times, I'm not so clear on where my feelings about a child are coming from, but I can feel myself getting into a negative pattern. When this happens, I've learned to pull back and go hunting for a positive. I am often surprised to observe a kindness that child has done. I write it down and it changes my mindset about that child.

◇   ◇   ◇   ◇   ◇

A boy in my room has occasional seizures. His parents and doctor have given me lots of information and support—but I'm still afraid of him. A few weeks ago, his mother came in all excited because he had taken his first steps over the weekend. I realized for the first time that he is a child first, and a child with seizures second. I began seeing things about him I had never seen before, such as his fascination with our class guinea pigs and how involved he gets in water play. I've decided to take a workshop about working with children with special needs to help me look beyond my fears and see him as he is.

Sometimes it only takes a slight change in perspective to turn negative feelings about a child into more positive ones. Judy tells about a time when she relied on her intuition about Danny, a boy in her third grade class, rather than focusing on Danny's negative behavior or the reactions he engendered in other staff.

When he entered my class in the fall, Danny already had developed a reputation as a bully, getting into daily fights during recess. Within the first weeks of school his fighting continued as did his trips to the principal's office. I sensed, from observing and talking with him, that he felt bad about this but he didn't have the skills and, more important, the confidence he needed to get through an entire recess without a fight. Children Danny's age need to feel competent and when they don't, their feelings of inferiority undermine their success. Danny expected to fail.

As I observed Danny each day, I felt uneasy. On the one hand, I was put off by his surliness—his negative attitude and quick dismissal of my or anyone else's efforts to engage him. Yet at the same time, I felt unsettled—distressed—by what seemed to be his inability to get along with others in the class and, for that matter, to do anything well. Despite the messages I was getting from other adults in the school, I forced myself to listen to the voice inside me that said, this child needs a chance to be special—to do something well. My uneasiness pushed me to take a risk, to reach out to him.

I suggested that he spend recess in the room with me rather than go outside. I told him that it was his choice, not a punishment, but a chance to get through a day without a trip to the office. I offered to show him a special way of painting that I had learned. At first he turned me down, showing his least attractive side. Just before lunch he reconsidered and said he would stay in. We had a really nice time painting together. He enjoyed mixing colors and discovered that he was quite a good painter. Painting became Danny's special talent in our classroom. He taught others how to use the painting technique, spent many recess periods in the room painting, and after awhile we displayed his artwork in the hallway to rave reviews from his peers and other teachers.

In the case of Danny, paying attention to uneasy feelings proved to be just what was needed to form a relationship and give Danny a way to be appreciated. When your feelings about a child are very strong, whether positive or negative, they are a sign to pay attention and observe that child, and your own reactions, more carefully.

Your Professional Expertise

As an educator you bring a great deal to the act of observing—your knowledge, your particular areas of interest and expertise, and your experience. You can rely on these assets and use them to help you learn about children and build relationships with them.

Listen to the comments from two teachers:

> I have a list of developmental guidelines in my head—a kind of mental checklist. When I observe children I tune into how they use their hands and their bodies, how they use language—how long their sentences are. My mental checklist is my lens and, because of my special ed background, my observations are very analytical. I think this makes me a good observer. But one thing I have to watch out for is that I'm not so analytical that I lose sight of the whole. As I observe to learn about each of their skills, I always have to keep in mind that they are not just children who possess a certain set of skills, but unique individuals whom I have to observe over time to really get to know.

✧   ✧   ✧   ✧   ✧

> I have spent many years developing my expertise in teaching children to be readers and writers. I tune in immediately to the strategies children use to read and where they are as developing writers. When my first graders are reading and writing, I don't think about trying to actively observe. I'm just doing it all the time—every minute. I feel like I know the right questions to ask them to extend their thinking. I have to work harder to observe children in other areas of the curriculum—subjects where I don't have the same comfort level.

We encourage you to rely on your professional expertise as you observe children. And as these teachers have shared, it is valuable to keep an open mind, knowing that when it comes to observing to learn about children, no one knows it all and we all have more to learn.

STRIVING FOR OBJECTIVITY

As you have seen, observing has a very human side. No one can be totally objective. However, you can increase your objectivity significantly by differentiating between what you actually see and hear—the facts, and what you think you see—your own opinions and interpretations of these actions.

For example, consider these two different observations of five-year-old Jason during choice time.

> 7/13: 11:00 a.m.—Jason chooses to read because he enjoys it.
>
> 7/13: 11:00 a.m.—Jason went straight to the reading area during choice time. Began reading Frog and Toad. After a few minutes he looked over to where Doug and Julie were building with blocks. I watched for a few minutes as he watched the children playing. I went over and asked him if he wanted to go play with them. He shook his head and went back to reading his book.

Though both records convey that Jason reads, the first gives only the teacher's impressions. Very often, we observe a child's behavior and think we know what is going on.

However, by describing a child's actions in detail, as illustrated by the second observation record, the teacher has enough information to ask questions that will lead to supporting Jason: How much time does Jason actually spend reading in the library corner versus watching the other children? Does he engage in other activities besides reading when given a choice? Does he ever approach children and join in an activity? Is there something I can do to help him feel more comfortable in other areas of the room? Consider these examples:

Jerome, a kindergarten teacher, has recorded this observation about Omar, who is drawing and writing about the class trip to the apple orchard.

> 2/13: Omar: Drawing and Writing
>
> Selects 3 crayons from box. Rolls them on table. Looks around. Picks up crayon from floor. Makes a few marks on paper. Walks to the window—back to table. Looks at Richard's paper. To Richard, "Whatchya drawing? I'm gonna make apples." Uses green crayon to draw a circle, pressing hard, scribbles in color.

Miriam, a kindergarten teacher, has recorded this observation about Justine working on a collage:

> 4/21: Justine: Art Table
>
> J is confused and frustrated. She is not relaxed or enjoying the assignment. After a few minutes she gets up and leaves the table, leaving the task incomplete.

What do you notice about the two observational records?

Jerome was objective. He noted what actually happened—what he saw and heard Omar do. Miriam focused on her interpretations of Justine's actions—what she thought Justine was thinking and feeling.

Can Miriam actually know if Justine was confused, frustrated, tense, or not enjoying the activity just from watching her? Instead of Miriam's interpretations becoming conclusions, they can be questions that require further exploration. For example, after observing, Miriam might wonder: Is Justine confused or frustrated? Did she not enjoy the task? If not, why not? These questions might prompt Miriam to engage Justine in conversation. Or, she might observe Justine using different materials to see if her behavior is the same or different.

When you record your observations, you can make room for your questions and interpretations. As we discussed earlier in this chapter, your impressions and feelings can add rich insights.

Just be sure to identify them as such. Some teachers divide their records into two parts, as illustrated in the example below. They write observations on one side, and on the other they note questions, concerns, and interpretations.

Notes	Interpretations
7/13: 11:00 a.m.—Jason went straight to the reading area during choice time. Began reading Frog and Toad. After a few minutes he looked over to where Doug and Julie were building with blocks. I watched for a few minutes as he watched the children playing. I went over and asked him if he wanted to go play with them. He shook his head and went back to reading his book.	Reading or avoiding approaching other children? Why not?

The strategies we offer below can help you be as objective and effective an observer as possible.

Tune in to individual children

The story of who children are—what makes them unique individuals—comes to light through the details you collect about them over time. As two teachers describe it:

Observation by observation, bit by bit, a picture of a child unfolds and continues to blossom throughout the year.

    ✧   ✧   ✧   ✧   ✧

Before I began using an observational assessment, I tended to get the big picture of things in my classroom. I always said that I knew my kids really well. I could tell you who talked a lot at circle time, who was quiet, who did the work, who always forgot assignments. But once I started to observe more, I realized how much I didn't know about them. I started paying attention more—noticing little details about what they said, how they interacted with each other, how they went about tasks. I can tell you really specific details about each child now.

Tuning in to each child and observing for details can be a challenge for at least two reasons. First, if your classroom is like our classrooms were, you're always on the go, answering at least two children's questions at once, helping another to find a missing puzzle piece, and constantly monitoring to be sure that everyone is safe and engaged. Having so many demands on your time can make it difficult to focus and, as a result, can lead to superficial observations. In addition, because you spend the majority of your waking hours in your classroom with the same children, it can be hard to pay close attention to what you see all the time.

Observing details requires slowing down and looking with care. Consider the contrast between Ms. Jennings's intentions and the results of her actions in the examples below.

When Brian calls Ms. Jennings over to show her his painting, she rushes over, glances at it quickly, and says, "Nice job, Brian," as she hurries off to Laurie, who has asked for help with the computer. In her haste, she misses an important opportunity to observe and use what she sees to connect with Brian and have a meaningful conversation about his work.

Now imagine that Ms. Jennings slows down for a moment, takes a careful look at Brian's painting, and says, "Brian tell me about your painting. What do you like about it?" She waits while he considers his response. Through this interaction Ms. Jennings shows her sincere interest in Brian's work and asks for his opinions. Brian has a chance to feel good about himself and reflect on his creation because Ms. Jennings took a moment to tune into Brian and his work.

Describe rather than label children's behavior

All of us rely on labeling words such as shy, aggressive, helpful, cooperative, annoying to describe people and actions because labels are quick and easy to use. They are right there, on the tip of our tongues. Consider this teacher's description of a child: "Tiara is withdrawn."

 Based on this teacher's words, what do you imagine Tiara is like?

Each of us has social constructions or meanings for words that are based on our experiences and our culture. However, the behavior(s) that cause us to label a child can reflect many different meanings. Consider the following behaviors and reasons why a teacher might describe a child as withdrawn:

✦ she was quiet because she needs some help getting adjusted to a new situation;

✦ she was playing alone because she needs to learn strategies for engaging with other children;

✦ she was tired because she didn't sleep well the night before; or

✦ she was sad because her cat died recently.

As you can see, labeling a child as withdrawn could be misleading. Moreover, your feelings and attitudes about what "withdrawn" means determine your response.

Earlier in this chapter we discussed how assumptions trigger scripts that affect children's behavior and the attitudes of other children—and even adults—around them. Let's think about how this might work with Tiara:

What might you say or do when you see her sitting away from a group of children, head down, playing with some colored cubes? How might she respond? What will the other children learn about Tiara based on your actions or comments? How might they then behave toward her? What if you had a conference with Tiara's parents and described her as "withdrawn" rather than describing the behaviors that led you to that conclusion? How might they feel about Tiara? About you?

As you can see, labels can have a powerful ripple effect on a child's self-esteem and the attitudes of others toward that child. Labels do not reveal the specific characteristics that make each child unique.

Instead of using the word "withdrawn" to describe Tiara, imagine what you can learn about her by taking a little more time and using a few more words to elaborate on the behaviors you see that lead you to say she is withdrawn. For example, observations of Tiara watching but not speaking may lead you to discover that she does not know how to enter a group. Asking her parents how much she interacts at home may give you a picture of a very animated child interacting easily with her siblings.

What you can learn about a child is endless. The point is, when you use labels you limit the possibilities, which also limits your ability to get to know a child better and to support that child's success as a learner.

Listen to children

We often think we know how children feel or what they are thinking just from watching them. But because we can't be inside a child's mind, we can never know for sure. So what do we do? One solution is to go directly to the source. Children can be an amazing source of information about what they are thinking or feeling—if we just take the time to listen and ask questions.

As you'll see in the following examples, listening can take varied forms, depending on the age of a child and the situation. In the two examples below, teachers tell about listening to children who didn't say a word. They are learning about children by listening to them and reading the meaning of their expressions, gestures, and how they move:

> Vanessa, who just turned four months old last week, is a new child in our program. Yesterday she was fussy and I figured she was tired. I laid her in her crib and gently patted her back like I do with other babies. Inch by inch, she began squinching up away from my hand toward the corner of the crib. I think she may be one of those kids who is sensitive to touch. I'm going to talk with her parents and observe to see if I'm right.

✧   ✧   ✧   ✧   ✧

> Arrival is a really important observation time for me. I observe kids as they come into the room in the morning. I look to see if they have a certain look—are they scowling, do they seem tired? I decide just how to respond. Sometimes I will take the child aside and say, so what's going on. Usually this helps a lot. But other times, I don't ask questions. Like with Jasmine. The other day she came in looking really upset. I decided that she needed a little extra attention and maybe some TLC. I didn't know what was wrong but, knowing her, asking wouldn't be the way to go. So, I greeted her warmly and suggested that when she was ready, perhaps she could feed the fish. As the morning wore on, she relaxed and settled into the day.

Group discussions and one-on-one conversations are only two of the many opportunities to learn who children are and what they know by listening to them. These examples illustrate how teachers learn by listening to children:

> Tiffany is four. She was busily at work in dramatic play. She and two other children were using props to play "firehouse." Tiffany

declared with authority, "Uh oh, that's the alarm. Hey you guys, put on your coats and boots. We better get the truck ready and get out of here in a hurry." Tiff rarely speaks up in group discussions, so I had no idea how much she had learned during our trip to the fire station. It was just one of those lucky moments that I happened to be listening while they were in dramatic play.

     ◇   ◇   ◇   ◇   ◇

As children work I wander around and sort of eavesdrop on their conversations. I am always amazed by how much they learn from each other. The other day, while working on their math, Shawna was giving Marie advice about how to settle a fight with Jocelyn. I was really impressed with Shawna's suggestions and with how thoughtfully Marie was listening. I wouldn't have pegged Shawna as one to give such good advice.

Learn from families

Families can help you get a clearer picture of their child by sharing information and responding to insights and questions based on what you observe.

You and families each bring different sets of information to your relationship. You have worked with many children of similar ages over the years. You know about general patterns of child development and have developed a collection of strategies to support children's learning. Parents or other family members focus on "their" child. They know the specific information about that one special child in their life. For example, they know about their child's culture, preferences, fears, and how their child responds in certain situations at home. To know a child, you need both sets of information. But you will never know what a family knows unless you exchange information, ask questions, and listen to one another. Like the teacher below, you may be surprised at what you learn:

When Nicky came in on Tuesday, we noticed his gait had a peculiar swing to it. We watched and began worrying that maybe he had developed some sort of neurological problem. That afternoon, Nicky's father came to pick him up. I asked him how things were going at home and he started talking about repairing the deck on his father's boat. Nicky had spent the long weekend with his grandparents who live on a houseboat, and his gait reflected the gentle rock of the boat!

When you share observations with parents you can sharpen your picture of a child by validating, expanding, or calling into question something you have seen.

 Remember Rami and Claudia (page 31)? How do you think Rami's school experience would have been different if Claudia had been able to hear what his mother was saying and as a result put aside her assumptions and seen Rami's behavior in a new way?

Communicating effectively with parents doesn't mean you have to be best friends, or even like one another—though that certainly makes life easier. What it does mean is that you have to see yourselves as partners with the child's best interests as your shared concern.

This isn't always easy. Sharing the care and education of children can stir up deep emotions, including jealousy, competition, and resentment. Have you ever had fleeting thoughts such as: "If this were my child, her clothes would be clean" or "If this parent were better at setting limits, his child wouldn't be disrupting the group"? We all have. These feelings usually stem from our attachment and commitment to children—qualities children need from their teachers. Yet they can interfere with the open communication between families and teachers that children also need. We're not suggesting you eliminate these feelings—you can't. We're simply encouraging you to be aware of them so they don't get in the way of the child's best interests.

Like all relationships, those with families take time to develop and require work to maintain. But they are well worth it.

Finally, keep track of how you are doing

Observing objectively requires ongoing vigilance. Using the strategies mentioned above will help, but they are no guarantee you will always see children for the unique individuals they are.

Because observing is such a personal endeavor, it is no wonder that sometimes it is more difficult to separate your experiences, feelings, and assumptions from what you are seeing. Being tired, upset about something, or under stress can make it a challenge to step back and be impartial.

To help you be as objective an observer as possible, we recommend regularly checking in to give yourself an "objectivity tune-up." Ask yourself:

☼ Have I gathered sufficient observational data to form a conclusion?

☼ Am I aware of how my feelings might be influencing what I'm seeing?

☼ Am I taking enough time before I label or interpret?

If you have doubts, enlist the assistance of a colleague. Ask that person to observe with you, then to confirm or call into question what you have seen. Even if you don't have doubts, observing with a colleague every now and then can help you be sure you are seeing what is, not just what you think is there. The children you teach deserve no less.

Teacher judgment and decision making form the core of good classroom practice. As we discuss later in the book, you make on-the-spot judgments and decisions throughout the day. But, when making judgments about children—who they are, what they know, and how they learn best—it is important to make informed judgments that are based on sufficient evidence. Descriptive information and information collected by talking with children and their families provides you with the evidence you need to feel confident that your judgments are accurate.

SUMMING UP

We can never eliminate the personal side of observing, nor would
that be a good idea. At the same time, you need to be aware of it
because what you bring to observing shapes how you see children
and families, which in turn, affects your relationships with them and
the decisions you make. To help you be sure that your pictures of
children and your relationships with them reflect reality rather than
your assumptions about them:

- ○ **Be aware of what you bring to observing**—your
  culture, temperament, interests, feelings, and professional
  expertise. This will increase the chances that your observations
  will give you insight into who children are and that your relationships with them will be authentic.

- ○ **Strive for objectivity**. Strategies to help you be an objective
  and effective observer include tuning into individual children,
  describing rather than labeling children's behavior, listening to
  children, learning from families, and keeping track of how you
  are doing by giving yourself an "objectivity tune-up."

In the next chapter, we look at guidelines for effective observation.

Guidelines for Effective Observation

W hat do you think about when you hear the word observing? When we ask teachers how they picture "classroom observation," they usually describe a teacher or caregiver sitting or standing with clipboard in hand, showing little or no facial expression, ignoring comments and social overtures from the children. Many of us see ourselves outside the action, clipboard in hand, taking notes. As you will see, this is only one way to observe. There are many other ways to learn about children. You can:

○ watch them with family members when they arrive and at the end of the day;

○ observe them as they engage in daily routines, jotting down what they do or say;

○ watch them as they play and work with materials and other children, making some notes about what you see;

○ talk with them about what they are doing or making— for example, when they explore playdough, paint, write, or build with blocks;

○ ask questions that encourage them to describe their thinking and listen carefully to their responses;

○ listen as they talk with others informally and during group discussions, jotting down notes about what they say;

○ study their work (e.g., projects, constructions, drawings, writing, journals);

○ observe them during home visits; and

○ talk with family members to learn their children's likes and dislikes or special interests.

These ways of learning about children point to four guidelines for effective observation: observe over time; watch children in varied situations; keep track of what you observe; and observe in and out of the action.

OBSERVE OVER TIME

One observation can never give you a complete picture. Only after observing over time are you able to see a child's growth and progress. Consider this analogy:

Imagine for a moment that you are planting daffodil bulbs. Someone passes by and asks you what you're doing. Amazingly enough, the passerby has never seen a daffodil before. You show her the bulb and she observes it carefully. She sees something round and brown with a little shoot sticking out. You encourage her to pass by a few more times to study the daffodil: first in the early spring to see the long green leaves and the tightly closed bloom; then perhaps a week or two later to see the bright yellow blossom; and maybe one month later to see drooping leaves. Despite the passerby's one-time careful observation of the bulb, you know that she must observe the daffodil over time to see it grow and change.

The same holds true for children. Observing the same child more than once, over time, will enable you to see that child change and grow. More limited observation will only tell part of the story.

Each time you observe a child, you learn something important. For example, you might watch a mobile infant using a chair to pull himself up. This event prompts you to double check nearby furniture for sharp corners and steadiness. Or you might see that a first grader uses her fingers to count to ten. As a result of this observation, the first grade teacher can build on the child's strategy of using fingers to show her how to count to 20. Each observational moment gives you information that you can use to help the child grow and learn.

A student teacher shared this story with us about Pam, age 7:

My first week of student teaching, there was a little girl who stood apart from the group, over behind the bookshelf during circle time. In my notes, I wrote: "Pam—Doesn't participate." Privately I thought she was really out of it. I was worried about her.

I asked my cooperating teacher, Alisa, why she didn't ask Pam to join the group. We talked about Pam's generally cautious temperament and her reluctance to join structured group activities. Alisa explained to me that sometimes the best way to support an individual child and the group is to ignore a behavior and proceed with the lesson.

We observed Pam for the next few weeks. To my surprise, I saw a child who was very engaged. Pam nodded yes when Alisa asked if everyone had read Chapter Two. She raised her hand and answered a question—all from her spot at the bookshelf. We observed that Pam interacted quite comfortably with individual children. It seemed to be the large-group, structured activities that threw her.

Then one day, about a month into the year, Pam came out from behind the bookshelf and sat on the floor in front of the shelf during a group discussion. A week later, Alisa patted the floor inviting Pam to sit next to her. Pam looked away, then back at Alisa and slowly walked over and sat down. She was quiet that day and the next. But by the end of the semester, when it was time for me to leave, Pam shared regularly in group time. This little girl I had been so concerned about was just fine.

If the student teacher had not observed over time, she would have never been alert to the subtle ways Pam was participating.

WATCH CHILDREN IN VARIED SITUATIONS

Think of how you act in different situations. In settings where you are comfortable, you may be outgoing and talkative. In other less familiar ones, you may hold back and be reluctant to share your thoughts. Children also behave differently in varied situations. For example, 11-month-old Melissa falls asleep easily on the cushions in the reading corner, but puts up a struggle when her caregiver tries to lay her down in her crib for a nap. Craig, age five, comes to life outdoors, taking initiative in inventing games and organizing his friends. Eight-year-old Khalan speaks easily to friends and family at home, but remains quiet and reserved in the classroom.

Observing in different situations gives us a more complete understanding of who a child is and what that child knows and can do. As one teacher said:

> I love putting all the information together and creating a picture of the child. After I started consciously trying to observe in different situations and over time, I realized I had been blind and not seeing the whole.

What factors should you consider as you attempt to observe children in varied situations? Here are a few suggestions.

Social Settings

The size of a group and the child's familiarity with group members are likely to influence behavior. Consider these examples. Jenny, age three, speaks easily with her teacher when they read a story alone together, but is shy and reserved when asked a question in front of her peers. On a class field trip, eight-year-old

Paul readily asks the naturalist (someone he has never met before) questions about the fish, whereas Justin, usually bursting with questions for his teacher or classmates, is very quiet.

Time of Day

You have probably noticed that children behave differently at different times during the day. For example, think about the infant who is alert in the morning and more drowsy in the afternoon. Or, a tired and grumpy four-year-old who won't join the group for a story first thing in the morning, but is an eager group participant after snack.

Individual Preferences

Children's preferences, like ours, affect their comfort level and attitude and, thus, their behavior. Some children like to build, others prefer painting, still others are most comfortable talking and writing. Some light up at a cooking activity and others when read to aloud. To observe what children know and can do, we have to get to know their preferences and then watch them in these situations. Consider this example from Maria, a kindergarten teacher:

> I was convinced that Shaquin had a language problem because she rarely spoke during group time, one-on-one, or even in small groups. When she did, it was one or two words, no complete sentences, and very limited vocabulary. One day I was observing the children in dramatic play where they had set up a beauty parlor. I heard Shaquin chatting away enthusiastically, questioning one of her customers: "How short should I cut your hair? Do you want me to dye it lighter than last time? On reflection I realized that Shaquin often chose dramatic play during work time and was more verbal doing something she enjoys.

Degree of Choice

Sometimes children's behavior is affected by whether they have chosen an activity. When children select activities they are interested in and care about, they are likely to engage more readily and with greater enthusiasm than teacher-directed activities as this story from a kindergarten teacher shows:

> I was preparing for a family conference and I couldn't think of anything positive to say about Derrek. I knew my concerns clearly and planned to share with his mother that he was contrary, obstinate, and unwilling to follow my directions—obviously not using those words! I forced myself to study my observation notes and samples of his work. Most of my notes described his behavior problems. However, I did notice a few examples of carefully completed work, particularly drawings he had made during choice time and put into his portfolio. One drawing was a very detailed picture of a ship—he used pencil and crayons. I didn't think he had such well-developed fine motor skills because when I ask him to write, mostly he scribbles. I realized then that I had to work on giving Derrek more choices and control over his work, even when I'm directing the activity. I also decided to share the drawing with his mom at the beginning of the conference.

Level of Competence

Children who feel competent are more likely to experiment and engage in new activities. For example, 23-month-old Elliot, who has parents and caregivers who give him many opportunities to experience success, climbs to the top of the new slide in the park and calls out, "Me do it!" First grader Yi-Ping, who also has developed a sense of confidence, volunteers to read aloud from a new book.

Try observing one or two children for a few days, noting how their behaviors vary depending on the situation. Are their actions the same regardless of the situation? Or do they vary depending on whom they are interacting with, where they are, and the time of day? Are their actions affected by their preferences, whether they have chosen an activity, and how confident or competent they feel to complete the activity?

KEEP TRACK OF WHAT YOU OBSERVE

Writing something down makes you pay attention to it. Recording your observations will help you tune into nuance and detail that you might otherwise miss. When you write things down, you can keep track of a child's development over time. You can identify and reflect on patterns that will give you a clearer picture of the whole child. Here's what some caregivers, teachers, and family child care providers say about recording:

> My anecdotal notes are little glimpses into children's personalities, which, if I didn't write down, I wouldn't recall.

> Writing stuff down allows me to focus better on the child. I remember more details. I look at my notes and recall how long the situation lasted, how long the child stayed with a task. I write really brief notes—sometimes just a word or two.

If the thought of writing is intimidating for you, relax. Chapter 5 describes many different techniques you can use to document observations. We also want to point out that observing is valuable, whether or not you record what you see. As one caregiver said:

> I observe all the time without taking notes—it's all observing and all meaningful.

Remember, the goal is to be a careful observer so that you get to know children well. Writing something down makes you more intentional. But don't feel as if you have to write a great deal—a few words, a phrase or two—will help you keep track of what you observe. Give yourself little assignments so that your recording has a purpose and doesn't feel overwhelming. For example, observe and record examples of ways children use language to describe. Or, decide to pay attention to children's scientific thinking. Try to record the type of questions children ask or the predictions they make. The key is to focus on something you find interesting or that you need to know.

Observe In and Out of the Action

Most often, we think of observing as happening when we are not a part of classroom activities. The benefit of stepping out of the action is that you can temporarily put down all the balls you are juggling and focus on who or what you are observing. It doesn't have to take a great deal of time. You will be surprised by how much data you can collect by taking three to five minutes to observe one or two children a few times each week.

However, stepping out of the action is often not feasible in the midst of a busy child care setting or classroom. Having other options in mind can help you observe more regularly. Here are two other approaches.

Observe While Participating in the Action

You are typically in the midst of the action. You might be changing a diaper, making a batch of playdough with a small group of two-year-olds, conferring with a student about his writing, guiding a small group through a math lesson, or having a discussion with your class about transportation in your city.

At the same time, you are watching children, listening to them, taking mental notes about who is doing what, and asking questions that extend children's learning and thinking. Clearly, you are gathering a wealth of information. The first challenge you face when you are at your busiest is how to focus enough on what you're observing so that you will remember some of it. Even at these very busy times, we encourage you to give yourself permission to slow down a bit, take a deep breath, and notice more consciously what one child is doing, even if you miss another child's activities.

A second challenge is figuring out how you can record some of what you see so that you don't have to rely solely on your memory. In this situation you can probably only record a few words, or make check marks or other symbols on a class list. But even if you don't get to write something down, just being more conscious will help you get to know your children better. The next chapter offers many different ideas about how to capture a quick note when you are participating in the action.

Reflect on the Action after the Fact and Make Some Notes

Reflecting after the fact is often the most practical way to record what you see and hear in a busy center or classroom. You probably make mental notes in the midst of the action all the time. By taking a few minutes during a break in the day (e.g., during rest time, quiet reading, or journal time) or at the end of the day, you can record brief notes about events that occurred. Recall how various children responded to the sights and sounds of a neighborhood walk, the strategies children used to solve math problems, or children's comments during a discussion about recycling.

A preschool teacher shares how she reflects after the fact:

I take a lot of photographs during the course of the week. I revisit them with the children and alone. I write things down as I look at the photos when I have time during the day or at the end of the day.

If you work with preschool and school-age children, you probably spend time reviewing their work at the end of the day or week. Make some notes about what you see. Ask yourself what the work shows. Looking at the work will remind you of events related to its creation. You are likely to recall:

- how the child went about the task,
- the child's interest level,
- whether the child worked alone or with others, or
- what else was happening in the classroom at the time.

To be a successful observer, we must broaden our image of observing beyond watching from the sidelines to include observing and recording while participating with children and reflecting and jotting down notes after the fact.

SUMMING UP

We learn about children by carefully watching them, listening to them, and studying their work. Watching and listening to them helps us understand what they are feeling, learning, and thinking. Here are four guidelines to help you be an effective observer:

○ **Observe over time.** Observing the same child over time enables you to see that child change and grow.

○ **Watch children in varied situations.** Like you, children may act differently according to the situation. Such factors as the social setting, time of day, individual preferences, degree of choice, and level of competence may influence a child's behavior.

○ **Keep track of what you see.** This will help you become a more intentional observer, notice patterns, and obtain a more complete picture of the child.

○ **Observe in and out of the action.** Don't limit yourself by thinking that you can only observe when you step out of the action. Observe while participating in the action, reflect on the action after the fact, and/or make some notes.

The next chapter discusses the many decisions you make every day about observing, including selecting your "tools of the trade."

CHAPTER 5

Becoming a Skilled Observer

Effective observing doesn't just happen. It involves thoughtful planning—an ongoing process of asking questions and making decisions. "How can you expect me to stop and think about when and how to observe in the middle of a busy day when I have hundreds of other things to think about?" you may ask. We don't. We have learned that effective observing requires planning: making decisions in advance about what and how you want to observe.

As you become a more experienced observer, your questioning, decision making, and planning become second nature—a part of your ongoing thinking process. There will be times when you have to pause and struggle a bit to be sure you get the information and insight you need. But the wonderful thing about observing is that it is (at least it should be) an ongoing practice, so if you miss something today you can catch it tomorrow.

This chapter identifies and discusses questions to consider and decisions to make with regard to effective observing. Being aware of these questions and thinking about them ahead of time will increase your chances of finding out what you want to know about children, families, and/or yourself as a teacher.

Don't be surprised to discover you are asking yourself these questions every day—perhaps without realizing it.

- ☼ What do I want to find out?

- ☼ When and where should I observe to get the information I need?

- ☼ How do I record what I observe?

- ☼ How do I organize the information I collect?

What Do I Want to Find Out?

As a teacher, you are aware of and open to what is going on around you. You are engaged in an ongoing process of asking questions, gathering information, and reflecting on and hypothesizing about what you observe. You will recall that in Chapter 2 we discussed questions that help you get to know children in order to build relationships with them. We described observation as the process of asking questions and answering questions. The questions you ask change continually, depending on a variety of factors including how well you know a child, the child's stage of development, and the specific issues of a child or family.

Sometimes you will know who or what you want to learn more about and ask yourself very clear questions to guide your observing. The chart on the opposite page has some examples of these questions.

Other times, your questions may be harder to put into words—or you may not even be aware that you have a question. Caregivers and teachers we've spoken with describe observing in these instances as "open observing," as trying "to get a feel for a child," "to better understand what a child is experiencing," and "to get a sense of what is going on." Listen as two teachers describe this type of observing:

TO LEARN MORE ABOUT:	YOU MAY ASK QUESTIONS SUCH AS:
An individual child	○ What is this child's temperament? ○ How does this child interact with others? ○ What does Johnny know about monarch butterflies?
A family	○ How does Rachita's family promote her language development? ○ How does a family feel about promoting independence (e.g., does Kyle's mother encourage him to put on and fasten his own coat or does she do it for him to be nurturing)? ○ How involved is Baili's family in helping her do her homework?
Particular skills or content	○ How can the toddlers participate in lunchtime? ○ What do children know about patterns? ○ In what ways are children using revision strategies in their writing?
Group dynamics	○ How is the transition between lunch and naptime going? ○ Who is working/playing with whom during morning center time? ○ What's going on with the group during recess that is causing so many kids to come back to the room angry?
The physical environment	○ How can I arrange the shelves so children can make clear choices about what they want to play with? ○ How can I change the block area to avoid so many toppled buildings and arguments during work times? ○ How can I modify the environment to promote more collaborative group work?
The effectiveness of your planning, interactions, and instruction	○ How do the children respond to the way I set limits? ○ How do the children respond to the stories I'm reading to them? ○ Did children understand the directions I gave for completing their science projects?

You are open to what a child may bring, getting inside his head, by noticing all of the child's cues.

You come in with a blank picture. You observe and the pieces come together. You need to be open to what you see. As you watch and interact, a relationship forms. Then you can observe for particulars. With free-form observing, you gain greater appreciation of how kids see the world—of their individual styles and your impact on kids. It helps you see through their eyes—to see them grow.

We know from our own experience that this "open" observing is a way of being with children. As described in Chapter 2, as teachers observe, they engage with children and build relationships with them. Teachers speak passionately about the experience. "You're connected by an invisible thread," one told us. In the words of another, "It is as if you feel a child. You become a part of them, they become a part of you."

We encourage you to consider the idea that when you observe in this way, you are asking a question, even if you haven't put it into words. Your question may be as open as "Who is this child?" or "How are things going?" or "That looks interesting, what's happening here?"—but it is still a question.

Putting what you want to learn into a question provides you with a clear purpose as an observer. It is also the heart of assessment. As one family child care provider told us:

It really helps me see that when I'm observing, I'm doing important work.

Being aware of your question doesn't have to detract from the wonder of what you see or feel as you get to know a child. Indeed, it often makes the experience richer and more gratifying. You will know that your observation is not something that just happened. Instead, your skills as an observer and listener combine with your knowledge of child development and allow you to watch as individual children discover something new about the world around them.

You should realize that stating a question doesn't guarantee that you will find the answer immediately. Indeed, there are bound to be times when you can't see—at least in the short term—what you have learned. Other times you might feel slightly overwhelmed by images and information that don't immediately make sense. When this happens, keep watching. Continue reflecting and hypothesizing about what you have noticed. Observe again. Eventually the information you collect will become part of a bigger picture and lead to new questions and new observations.

Think about your most recent observations. What are some of the questions you have been trying to answer?

WHEN AND WHERE SHOULD I OBSERVE?

There will be times when you can plan when and where to observe. For example, if you want to see how 18-month-old Louis is handling separation, observe him at the beginning and end of the day when his grandmother drops him off and picks him up. To discover what Amanda, age 4, knows about patterns, you can introduce pattern blocks to her during choice time. And to help you assess the sense of community among your second graders, you can observe interaction during group discussion and work time.

Sometimes you figure out the when and where on the spur of the moment—for example, when you observe because you see or hear something that strikes you as curious or simply because you have a free minute. Because children express what they are feeling and learning throughout the day, being open—to the expected and unexpected—means that you catch many small moments that add up to a greater understanding of the children you care so much about. As you help a child get ready for a nap, you may glance up to see Louis shoring up his sense of connection with home as he wanders over to the family pictures hanging on the wall and touches the one of his mother. Amanda's ability to duplicate patterns may be demonstrated when she arranges raisins and pretzel sticks on her placemat at snack time. Or a developing sense of community may be revealed when you overhear three children talking after recess about how to include other children in tomorrow's kickball game. Observing spontaneously can reveal a great deal of information about children.

Include planning for observation as part of your daily and weekly schedule. We're not suggesting a great deal of extra writing. For example, if you want to know more about how Louis handles separation throughout the day, jot down "Louis— separation?" on Monday and Wednesday. During those days, keep an eye on him to see if he is playing peek-a-boo, calling home on the toy phone, talking about his parents, or engaging in any other behaviors that help toddlers feel some control over hellos and good-byes and connected with those they love. If you are wondering what Amanda knows about measurement, jot down "Amanda—measuring" next to the cooking activity you have planned for Thursday. These small reminders will help you find out what you want to know.

This illustration shows a segment of a first grade teacher's plan book. She includes plans for

4/5	Monday
8:15	Morning meeting - - intro measuring "Why do you think we have rulers and other measuring tools?" (record comments on chart)
8:30	Math work time - (make grid) - using string & non-standard unit of choice, measure body lengths.
9:10	Writers workshop - check in w/ Ryan, Brett, Lori, She Kaya
10:00	Library - who has a plan? - Jessica, Trey, Bobby ???

observation by making notes to remind her of what or whom she wants to observe. On Monday, she plans to introduce the week's unit on measurement during the morning meeting. She records children's responses on a chart, keeping track of who said what by placing children's initials next to their name. Her note "make grid" is a reminder that she needs to make a matrix (see pp. 76–77) to observe and document specific skills. After reviewing some of her observational notes from the previous week, she decides to check in with children she hasn't conferenced with for two weeks. When the children go to the library, her observations are focused by her question, "Who has a plan?"

How Do I Record What I Observe?

There are many ways to record observational data. Each technique makes different demands on your time and energy, and each provides a different kind of information. The decision about what methods to use depends on what you want to learn, the activities children are engaged in, and your responsibilities at the time you are observing. And, of course, how you record must match your personal style. This section provides you with a variety of options and highlights ways teachers have used them successfully.

As you can see from the comments of these two teachers, some use many methods and others rely on only one or two:

> I use all different methods and tools, depending on what and when I'm observing. Mostly I grab stickies and just jot down a quick note so I can remember it later.

✿   ✿   ✿   ✿   ✿

> I keep a small spiral notebook with me all the time and jot down what I see.

One first grade teacher told us:

When I have a conversation with a child that I want to remember, I need to make a note—I'll write down a few words so I don't forget what we talked about—otherwise it's gone. When I'm planning lessons I make grids. I write the names of the kids I want to observe and list four or five things I want to observe for. Doing this helps my observations stay focused.

Overall, most caregivers and teachers say they use a few different methods, rather than just one. For example, when observing a child's mood, thinking process, method for solving a problem, way of using materials, and quality of interactions with others, select a method that allows for some descriptive writing. On the other hand, if you simply want to record the materials a child selects to help solve a math problem, or the colors a child names accurately, it is more efficient to use a method that allows you to make checks or tally marks.

When you are working one-on-one with a child, reading a book together, or having a writing conference, you have the time to take rich notes that describe the child's actions and words. However, when circulating to guide children's learning during a science activity, making quick check marks on a matrix is easier to manage.

We describe several different methods below and show some examples of each.

Brief Notes

Brief notes, the most common way teachers record their observations, are quick written records that serve as a reminder of observed events. Teachers typically record these notes on Post-its®, index cards, mailing labels, or whatever piece of paper happens to be close at hand.

Brief notes on mailing labels

A preschool teacher jotted these brief notes about the children she teaches on a sheet of mailing labels she keeps handy on a clipboard. At the end of the week she'll peel the labels off and place each label in that child's section of a binder she uses to store her observations.

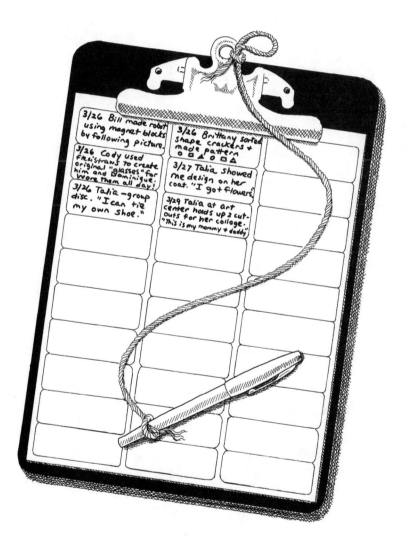

Brief notes on index cards

A first grade teacher wrote a set of brief notes during one week to keep track of Alex's reading and writing. She records notes about all of her students on index cards attached to a file folder. When she fills up a card, she transfers it to her file on that child and replaces it with a new card.

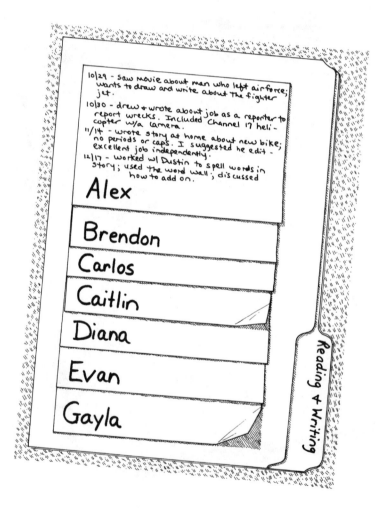

10/29 - Saw movie about man who left air force; wants to draw and write about the fighter jet.

10/30 - drew + wrote about job as a reporter to report wrecks. Included Channel 17 heli-copter w/a camera.

11/14 - wrote story at home about new bike; no periods or caps. I suggested he edit - excellent job independently.

12/17 - worked w/ Dustin to spell words in story; used the word wall; discussed how to add on.

Alex

Brendon

Carlos

Caitlin

Diana

Evan

Gayla

Reading + Writing

Brief notes on a daily log

An infant/toddler caregiver created this form to use to exchange news and observations with families about their child's day.[3]

DAILY LOG

Child's name: __Jason__   Date: __11/3__

NEWS FROM HOME -
How did your child sleep last night?
Well __X__ Woke up in the night _____ How much? __A few__
When did your child last eat? __7:00__
__spoonfuls of cereal__
Who will pick up your child today? __Grandma__ When? __5:00__
Medication today? Yes _____ No __X__
Special instructions: _____
Anything happening in your child's life we need to know?
__Jason's grandparents are visiting for__
__the week.__

NEWS FROM CHILDCARE -
Medication? Yes _____ No __X__   When? _____
Your child ate: __french toast__   When? __10:00 a.m.__
__sandwich and pear__   When? __11:30 a.m__
__peanut butter & crackers__   When? __3:00 p.m.__
                                            When? _____

Your child slept from: __12:30__ to __2:30__
                        _____ to _____

Your child had a b.m. Yes _____ No __X__
Today your child enjoyed: __Collecting stones in his pail,__
__watching a squirrel, doing a puzzle and going__
__through the obstacle course we made.__
Please remember to bring in : diapers _____ wipes _____
set of clean clothes _____ Other: __family photos for our album__

Thanks. See you tomorrow!

---

[3] Adapted with permission from J. Greenman and A. Stonehouse, *Prime Times: A Handbook for Excellence in Infant and Toddler Programs*, St. Paul, MN: Redleaf Press, 1996, p. 284.

Anecdotal Notes

Anecdotal notes are more detailed, narrative accounts that describe a particular event factually. Often they are created by jotting down brief notes and adding details later. The following illustration is an anecdotal record from an infant caregiver who observed Victor's (12 months) reunion with his father at the end of the day.

Victor	4/29

V. is spinning a knob on the busy box and vocalizing. He pulls himself up to stand on the snack table, then gets down on all fours and crawls to the toy shelf. Still vocalizing, he heads back towards the busy box and comes face to face with his dad's legs. He quiets, sits, looks up at Dad, smiles, then turns away. Dad bends down and touches his cheek. V. raises his arms to be picked up. Dad lifts him off the floor and V. goes into his arms willingly, clutching Dad's jacket in one fist.

Here is an example of an anecdote describing several children.

●	Obs. for 4 min. Children observed:
	During Center Time Shelby, Maddy,
	          Andrea, Shanese,
	          Desiree + Teresse

Daily Observation

11/2

    Maddy and Shelby decided to put on a puppet show. Maddy directed Andrea, Shanese, Desiree, and Teresse where to sit. They sat where she directed them. Teresse got up and moved to the rocking chair, saying over and over, "I can't see." Maddy opened the curtains of the puppet stage and she and Shelby performed the story of the Little Red Riding Hood. As Shelby moved the puppets, she knocked down some props on the stage. Maddy declared, "Shelby! Now look." Shelby quickly picked them up. Shelby was Little Red Riding Hood; Maddy was mom. When they finished acting out the story, Desiree said, "I want to see it again." Teresse said, "I want to see it tomorrow." Maddy said, "I'm not going to do it again until you're all sitting down the right way. She waited until all the girls were seated. They began the puppet play again. Teresse stayed and listened.

Running Records

Running records are detailed narrative accounts of behavior recorded in a sequential manner, exactly as it happens. They include all behavior that occurs within a given time frame. Like anecdotal notes, they provide rich information, but require you to step out of the action.

In this example, a second grade teacher observes David working at the classroom bookstore, then reflects on what she has learned and how she will use this information. She wanted this degree of detail to help her prepare for a conference with David's family.

> David   11/2
>
> David is standing by the cash register in our classroom book store. Nikki comes over with two books — one for 10¢ and one for 30¢. She hands the books to David, who looks at the prices on each. He looks up for a moment, looks back at the books, and then says to Nikki, "40¢ please."

> 11/2 cont.
>
> David
>
> She pulls a few coins out of her pocket and stands looking at them. He looks in her hand and points to a quarter, a dime, and a nickel saying, "25¢, 35¢, 40¢." She gives him the three coins and takes her books. "Have a nice day," David says. (David has it! Needs more challenging, higher-level, multistep problems.)

Reading running records

A reading running record is a formal way to monitor children's reading behaviors by recording exactly what the child does and says while reading.[4] In particular, it is a way to learn about the particular reading strategies a child uses to understand the story (e.g., picture or phonetic cues, self-correction, etc.). Reading running records can be used for many purposes, including:

- ✿ documenting behavior for later reflection,

- ✿ identifying the reading strategies a child uses,

- ✿ determining the child's reading level to help with book selection,

- ✿ identifying next instructional steps,

- ✿ grouping students,

- ✿ monitoring progress, and

- ✿ making decisions about referrals for additional support or evaluation.

There are different ways to document children's behaviors using a reading running record. In some cases, teachers have a copy of the text the child is reading. Or teachers use a code to keep track of exactly what the child reads. When doing reading running records, it is advisable to use a standard coding method that is easily interpreted by others reviewing the documentation. There are several books included under Resources that can help you learn to use this documentation strategy.

---

[4] M. Clay, *An Observation Survey of Early Literacy Achievement*, Portsmouth, NH: Heinemann, 1995, pp. 20–42.

Matrices

A matrix or a grid is a way to record a word, a very brief note, or a rating for a few children or for the entire class. Names of students are listed on the left side of the page (or across the top). Space is allocated next to each name for comments. The matrix used by a second grade teacher to keep track of students' comments during daily literature discussions is shown below. Each day she uses a code to note who participates in the discussion. When she can, she tries to include comments. The class is reading *Stone Fox* by John Gardiner.

Literature Discussions   Week of 3/12 *Stone Fox*
A - active participation   P - participated somewhat
Q - quiet

Names		Comments/Reflections
Andrew	P	responded to Stevie about Gardiner's motive
Anthony	Q	
Bill	Q	
Collin	A	
Daniel	P	related personal story about being at a farm
Dayshonne	A	noted details about history/ compared to present day
Ebony	P	begins all w/ well, I think... comments not related to topic
Joshua	P	
Katie	Q	recalled details of yesterday's disc.
Keith	P	question about taxes
Lauren	Q	
Leah	P	recalls details; describes Willie's feelings
Matthew	P	
Nadine	Q	Does she get the story? Try to talk to her! 1-1
Nicole	P	
Richard	P	told personal story about his grandfather
Shawn	P	
Steven	abs	
Trayon	P	

Matrices are also used to focus observations on a set of skills, concepts, or behaviors typically listed across the top of the grid. The following illustration shows how a first grade teacher kept track of children's skills during a measurement activity. As a result of her observations, she determined that the next step for these children was a measurement activity with a more limited focus.

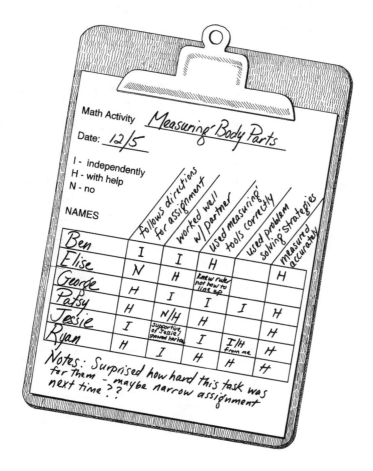

Math Activity _Measuring Body Parts_

Date: _12/5_

I - independently
H - with help
N - no

NAMES	Follows directions for assignment	worked well w/ partner	Used measuring tools correctly	used problem solving strategies	measured accurately
Ben	I	I	H		
Elise	N	H	knew ruler not how to line up		H
George	H	I	I	I	
Patsy	H	N/H	I		H
Jessie	I	Supportive of Jessie/showed harder	H		H
Ryan	H	I	I	I/H from me	H
			H	H	H

Notes: Surprised how hard this task was for them - maybe narrow assignment next time ??

Rating Scales

Rating scales are intended to show the degree to which children possess a certain skill. The illustration below shows a rating scale used by a kindergarten teacher at the beginning of the year to assess children's knowledge, skills, and participation level during daily opening activities. She includes students' names and a set of skills that she will focus on.

A rating scale allows you to record your observations as events occur. You can quickly record your judgment or evaluation of a child's performance on a particular occasion or as a summary of several observations. Remember that with a rating scale, however, you evaluate a complex behavior in a simple way and, therefore, see only one part of a bigger picture. Rely on other recording methods to capture the subtleties in children's behavior.

N - no P - partial C - competent	days of the week	yesterday/today/tomorrow	counting # of days in wk/m.	tens/ones	recognizes patterns	duplicates/extends patterns
Arletha	P	N				
Austin	C	C	P	P	C	P
Danielle	C	P	??	P	C	P
Dean	P	C	P	P	C	C
Emily	C	C	C	C	C	P
Gyrah	N	ck in w/her			C	C
Kiersten	P	P			P	P
Melissa	C	C	P	P		

Tallies

Tallies are used in two ways: to count the instances of a particular behavior or event and to count the instances of a behavior during a predetermined time interval. The following illustration shows how a preschool teacher used tallies on a matrix to record children's participation during daily group times. This method of recording helped her see patterns of children's involvement in activities. After two weeks of recording in this way, she reflected on her observations. She was surprised by how many children participated actively during story time. She decided to do some focused observing in small group situations of the children whose participation was limited during large group times. And, she planned to alter some of the morning circle activities to see if she could elicit greater participation.

Date: 3/21

	morning circle	discussions	story time	songs, music, poems
Alice	I	I	IIII	II
Brandon	IIII	II		
Brent	II	I	II	II
Bria				II
Candice	I	I	II	
Desmond	II	III	IIII II	III
Hollie	I		IIII	III
Jacky		I	IIIII	II
Jeffrey				I
Laquita		III	II	I
Pamela	II		II	
Paris				
Patrick	I	III	II	I
Raymond	II	I		II
Shawn		I		II
Steven			II	III
Torronda	II	I	II	
Yolanda	I		IIII	II
Zachary	IIIII I			

Diagrams, Sketches, and Photographs

When details of certain activities and projects are needed, photos, sketches, and diagrams may be the best way to capture information. As one teacher said:

> Taking photos helps jog my memory about a specific activity and what each child was doing. When I look at the photo, everything comes flooding back into my head.

It may be much quicker to draw a child's block building than to try to describe it in words. Older students can create these records themselves.

Audiotapes and Videotapes

Audiotapes and videotapes are excellent ways to capture children's language. Skits, puppet shows, storytelling, and reading aloud lend themselves to this method of documentation.

Teachers who observe regularly often use several different recording methods, selecting the method that best fits the particular questions they have and the situation in which they are observing. Equally important is finding a method that feels comfortable and natural.

How Do I Organize the Information I Collect?

If you are going to observe purposefully, you'll need a system that enables you not only to write down what you see but also to make order and learn from the written information you've gathered. Creating a system involves two steps:

 ✿ record your observations in a way that works for you, and

 ✿ organize and store your written observations so you can go back and learn from them.

Step One: Write Things Down in a Way That Works for You

When you choose tools that fit your needs and personal style, you are much more likely to record your observations. Some caregivers and teachers find jotting brief notes on index cards or Post-its works for them. Others use a variety of tools, including:

- ○ **Mailing labels.** Attach a sheet of mailing labels to a clipboard. You may want to pre-print them with children's names and the date.

- ○ **Legal pads.** In several key locations, place pads of paper with a pen or pencil attached so they'll always be where you need them.

- ○ **Butcher paper.** Hang butcher paper around the room and make notes directly on the paper or attach Post-its to it. Note: Teachers using this method are not concerned about children or parents reading their notes because they are factual.

- ○ **Masking tape.** Make notes on the tape, tear pieces off, and file in the child's file.

- ○ **Calendars.** Some teachers keep daily notes on a desk calendar. Others have a calendar for each child. Still others post on the wall a large monthly calendar drawn on butcher paper and record notes for themselves and parents of daily highlights.

- ○ **Tape recorders.** Dictate your observations into a tape recorder, but remember that taped information has to be transcribed.

- ○ **Still cameras.** Many teachers find taking a photograph a quick way to capture a record of an event or product.

- ○ **Video cameras.** These are useful tools for documenting children in action.

It may take time to figure out what works for you—but be patient during your process of trial and error. Writing down your observations helps you see and reflect on information that you can use to make moment-to-moment decisions, such as: "Should I pick up the rattle and hand it to Josie or let her reach for it herself?" "What can I ask to see whether Renee understands what she just read?" "Who can I have work on the city model with Frank to help him better understand scale?" "How can Jason's parents and I work best together to support his fragile self-esteem?"

Step Two: Organize and Store Your Written Observations So You Can Go Back and Learn from Them

The primary purpose of recording your observations and reviewing them later is to provide you with data for reflection. Teachers describe several different levels of reflection related to observing. The first occurs at the time you observe. Whether you record your observation or not, you act based on what you have seen. Your reflection and your decision about how to respond are almost simultaneous. If, for example, you know that Karla is most likely to bite when she gets in crowded spaces, you immediately steer her in another direction when you observe her heading into the refrigerator box house where two other toddlers are playing.

A second level of reflection occurs when you review your notes at the end of the day or week. Looking over your notes may help you decide to modify your plans for tomorrow or may give you ideas for next week. For example, as Tracy reviews her notes from writer's workshop for the week, she notices that several children have started to include dialogue in their stories. She decides that next week she will focus on dialogue during mini-lessons prior to writer's workshop.

This level of reflection allows you to distance yourself from everyday activities and understand the bigger picture of what is happening in your classroom. You may gain some insight about the pattern of a child's behavior by reviewing your observational notes from several days or a week. Or you may realize something new about your program. For example, after reviewing notes about several children who became involved in fights in the block area, you wonder how to rearrange the furniture to create a more workable space. Taking time to review your notes when you don't have to take immediate action allows you to examine the data more objectively, gain perspective, and make meaning of the information you have collected.

A third level of reflection takes place when you go back and analyze your notes over a longer period of time for purposes of formal assessment—when you need to write a report, prepare for a child study meeting, or conduct a family-teacher conference. This level allows you to recognize progress children have made. Sometimes it has the added benefit of showing you that troubling behaviors you were worried about two months ago have diminished or disappeared.

Review your notes regularly—we recommend weekly, twice a month at the least—to help you get the most from them. For the second and third levels of reflection, organization is essential. Sometimes it sounds easier to review and use information from observation notes than it actually is. Notes have an amazing ability to end up in "black holes"—pockets, filing cabinets, desk drawers—never to be seen again. And when they are sighted, they often tend to be in a state of confusion. During a recent workshop, a brave teacher held up a large jumble of Post-it® notes all stuck together in a clump. "I can find time to write my observations down," she said. "But I never get back to them." Laughter and a collective sigh of relief swept through the group. Clearly she's not alone. On the next few pages, we provide examples of systems for storing and organizing written observations that teachers, caregivers, and child care providers have shared with us.

I've made a folder for each child in which I keep my observations and notes from other teachers and parents. I'm now in the habit of spending 5–10 minutes each week filing my notes.

✧   ✧   ✧   ✧   ✧

I use index cards, which I store in a small file box. I create a section for each child. I keep the cards and a pen on the top of the bookshelf so they are handy. I stick the cards in my pocket as I write on them and, at the end of the day, file them under the correct name.

I keep a notebook for each baby in my room. Parents are welcome to take their child's book home and add observations from home. It works very well.

We have portfolios for each child that I made out of an accordion folder. In each portfolio, we keep observations and samples of that child's work that are shared with the child and his or her family. The child helps us choose which pieces of work to include. I keep my scribbled observations in a folder labeled with that child's name and stored in my filing cabinet.

✧　　✧　　✧　　✧　　✧

I hung a shoe bag in one of the closets of my family child care home. I label a section for each child and keep my notes about him or her right there.

In addition to your notes on individual children, think about how to store the observations you record on rating scales, matrices, and tallies used when working with a group. This is especially important if you work with children who are pre-school age and older. Many teachers find it helpful to keep a three-ring binder for these tools, which they organize by subject area. They then thumb through it as they reflect on individual children.

As you review your current system or consider what kind of system to develop, be sure it works for you. It should be convenient and easy to use. There should always be something to write with and on close at hand. Putting away your observations should be a simple task whether you do it when children are resting or out at music, at the end of each day, or at the end of the week. As you put away your notes, take a moment to scan them. If a question jumps out, jot it down in your plans to remind you about something you want to observe. Beware if you find a bunch of random notes growing in the corner: this is a sign that something is not working. Modify if necessary to keep your system from overwhelming you.

In the end, only two things about your system really count: Do you use your system? Does it help you better understand and respond to the children and families with whom you work?

SUMMING UP

Effective observing is an ongoing process of asking questions and making decisions. If you are aware of these questions and think about them ahead of time, you will increase your chances of finding out what you want to know about children, families, and/or yourself as a teacher:

- ☼ **What do I want to find out?** Putting what you want to learn into a question provides you with a clear purpose as an observer and often makes observing a richer, more gratifying experience.

- ☼ **When and where should I observe to get the information I want?** There will be times when you observe because you see or hear something that strikes you as curious or simply because you have a free moment. There will be other times when observing is planned rather than spontaneous.

- ☼ **How do I record what I observe?** There are many ways to record observational data, including brief notes, anecdotal notes, running records, rating scales, matrices, tallies, diagrams, sketches, and photographs. The method you use depends on what you want to learn, the activities children are engaged in, your responsibilities when you are observing, and your personal style.

- ☼ **How am I going to organize the information I collect?** As a purposeful observer, you need a system that enables you to write down what you see and allows you to make order and learn from the written information you gather. Creating a system involves two steps: one, write things down in a way that works for you, and two, organize and store your written information so you can go back and learn from it.

In Chapter 6, we examine how you apply the information you collect to the many decisions you make each day in your classroom.

Using What You Learn

Every decision you make about the environment, daily routines, and learning opportunities in your classroom affects children's learning. When you observe, you gain insights into children's strengths, knowledge, interests, and skills. You also discover barriers that may be inhibiting their success. You reflect on daily life in your program and make adaptations that enable children to overcome obstacles and build on what they know and can do well.

Throughout this book you have read stories that demonstrate how teachers use what they learn from observing to support children's learning. This chapter highlights specific ways you can use what you learn to create and maintain a quality program for the children you teach. We show how observing helps teachers individualize their program and instruction. In addition, we describe how observing enabled teachers to address challenging situations—health issues, disruptive behavior, and balancing individual and group needs. Finally, we offer two stories showing how observing can strengthen partnerships with families.

Stories in this chapter are presented in different formats. We use short examples to illustrate specific points and longer, more detailed stories shared by teachers to demonstrate how observing and reflecting over time leads to insights and interventions that worked.

INDIVIDUALIZING THE PROGRAM

Observing often helps caregivers and teachers individualize their program by adapting the environment and shaping daily routines to be more responsive to children's needs and strengths. As you read these examples, reflect on your own setting, what you observe there, and modifications you could make to support the children you work with each day.

Adapting the Environment

Observing gives you insight into how children use the environment. You can use this information to make changes in the environment that promote children's exploration, interactions, and learning. Consider the examples below.

In an infant-toddler program
At the end of the day, Karlene, an infant caregiver, reflects on what she has seen this past week:

> Over the past three days, Lynn, age 7 months, has been getting up on her hands and knees and rocking back and forth. Today, she put one hand in front of the other, moved a knee forward, rocked slightly back, and then crawled for several feet. She is the first child in our group to begin crawling.

As a result of this observation, Karlene decides to be extra careful regarding safety issues and explains:

> Though we are always mindful of safety, now that we have a crawler, I will crawl around the floor tomorrow and look once again for potential hazards. That way we'll be able to let Lynn explore the room freely.

In a kindergarten classroom

After observing more frequent disputes in the dramatic play area, a kindergarten teacher stepped back and noticed children were arguing over who could wear the hats and work gloves similar to those their parents wear in the fields.

In response, she enlarged the area and added more of these props. She also included some cardboard crates like those used for storing the broccoli currently being harvested. Since then, children have expanded their play to include delivering the broccoli to the store. With more space and props, the number of conflicts has diminished.

In a primary classroom

Richard, a teacher of six- and seven-year-olds, recently observed a pattern of children entering the art area, but leaving it almost immediately—even Carla and Ben, who love to paint. When he took a careful look at the art area, he saw containers of dried-up paint, and shelves crammed with trays, paper, and brushes and realized that one of the easels had been transformed into a private nook for reading. He commented:

> I was surprised and a little embarrassed about how messy things had gotten. No wonder kids didn't want to paint. Rather than handling it myself, I decided to present the kids with a problem-solving task. This morning, during meeting time, we looked at the art space together and made a plan to straighten it out. I predict that by next week, it will be back in full use.

Shaping Daily Routines

For children, the best thing about daily routines is that they happen each day, often several times a day. Because they happen at home too, routines are natural bridge-builders between home and the program. In addition, they are predictable enough to give children a sense of mastery over time. As children develop, routines offer new challenges and take on new meaning. Periodically observing during these routines means that these daily events will get the same attention and planning as all of the other valuable learning activities in your program.

In an infant-toddler program

A teacher of toddlers observed Ella during hellos and good-byes in an attempt to figure out how to make transitions easier for the two-year-old. One of his observations, recorded later, reads:

> Soon after arriving in the morning, Ella's father sits at the table and helps Ella climb into a chair. He takes pieces out of the puzzle and hands them one by one to Ella. She pushes them away three or four times. She then pushes the whole puzzle onto the floor and screams out, "No!" She screams, "No!" again when her father says he has to leave.

A few weeks later, the teacher made the following notes in Ella's book:

> This morning, Ella and her father went over to the bookshelf to choose a book to read before he left for work. I joined them and suggested Ella choose the book herself, which she proudly did. When it came time for her father to leave, I asked Ella if she wanted to wave to him from the window or walk him to the door. She chose to walk him to the door, where she gave him a big hug and said, "Bye, bye."

Reading through his notes, the teacher saw a pattern. Ella seems to manage better when she has some say in what is going on. He wondered if giving her realistic choices helps her feel a little more in control about the comings and goings in her life. The next day, he talked with his co-worker. They agreed: "We need to support Ella's growing sense of autonomy. We'll make a point to give her manageable choices—in the morning and throughout the day."

In a preschool program

Linda, a preschool teacher, observed that rest time was getting to be a struggle, especially with Nicholas, age 4. As Linda notes at the end of the week:

> Nicholas whines when I dim the lights and say it is time for a rest. He tells me, "I want to play, not sleep." On Tuesday, he lay down on his mat for a few minutes and began fidgeting, which soon escalated to his rolling off his mat and onto that of his neighbor. My struggling to get him to rest and be quiet totally defeats the purpose of rest time. We both end up frustrated.
>
> My solution has been to adapt rest time by letting Nicholas—and other children who don't sleep or nap—bring a quiet work activity with them to their mats, such as paper, crayons, and books. So far, so good. Yesterday, Nicholas drew an incredible picture of the zoo he visited over the weekend with his cousins—and even stayed on his mat.

In a third grade classroom

Pauline observed over time that her group was getting "antsy," and that children were spending more time fidgeting than listening to one another during group meetings. In response, she decided to raise the issue with the class. They decided to try to solve the problem by changing meeting seats each week.

A few weeks later, Pauline asked the children if they had observed a difference in group time behavior. Together they agreed that the situation had improved. To herself Pauline noted that by giving the students a chance to reflect and address the problem, they became more conscious of their behavior.

INDIVIDUALIZING INSTRUCTION

Children, like all of us, learn best when what they are learning is meaningful. When you observe, you learn about children's interests, strengths, and experiences. You can use this information to tailor instruction to the children in your classroom or program.

Building a Bridge with Home

When Korene's primary caregiver observes that Korene, age 7 months, smiles and bounces up and down whenever she hears music, she decides to ask her parents what kind of music they listen to at home. When they volunteer to bring in some jazz tapes, she enthusiastically accepts. She makes a point of listening to and enjoying Korene's family's favorite music, not only with her, but with the other children.

Following a Child's Interest

A preschool teacher noted on an index card:

> Leticia, age 3, whose home language is Russian, rarely speaks in school. One day we were talking about pets, and Leticia didn't say a word. But the next day, she and her mom came to school with Leticia's guinea pig from home.

The teacher explains:

> I found out Leticia understands more English than I thought she did. I knew I had to build on this to help her feel more comfortable talking at school. So, we wrote a story about Tiger, the guinea pig. Leticia worked on an illustration of what Tiger eats. I always have a camera on hand for moments like this, so I took some photos of Leticia, her mom, and Tiger. I gave one photo to Leticia to take home and kept some in our class photo album to remind Leticia and the other children of the special day Tiger came to school.

Shaping Instruction Based on a Child's Culture

Leslie, a first grade teacher in rural New England, overheard two children laughing at the accent of a new child in the group who was Vietnamese. She realized that living where they do, children's exposure to different ethnic and cultural groups is very limited, and that they need to learn more about different groups of people who live in the United States and across the world. She plans to bring in books, photos, and music reflecting different cultures. And to put everything in context, she is moving up the study on families she had planned for later in the year. As children discuss their families, she will highlight differences and similarities among them.

Using a Child's Interests to Encourage Independent Reading

Recently, a second grade teacher has been tallying how often she sees children actively engaged with books during quiet reading or choice time. After two weeks of observing, she noticed that there were no tally marks next to Kenny's name. An active six-year-old who excels in soccer and block building, Kenny wasn't spending time reading on his own. The closest he had come was to use books to make hideouts for the class rabbit.

In response, the teacher began looking in the library for a book about soccer—and was delighted when she found one with very simple text about second and third graders. It was a hit. Kenny has read *Soccer Sam* by Jean Marzollo three times on his own. She also borrowed *The Soccer Mystery* by Gertrude Chandler Warner and suggested to Kenny and his father that they might enjoy reading it together. On Friday, when the class visits the school library, she and Kenny are planning to look for more books about soccer and other sports.

Identifying a Health Issue

Have you every worked with a child whom you just didn't understand? No matter how you modified instruction, varied your schedule and routines, or changed activities, you didn't seem to be able to get a grasp on that child's experience. In these situations, purposeful observing can help you begin to identify the issue. Consider David's experience with Reggie.

David has been a kindergarten teacher for more than 15 years in a suburban public school system. He is relatively new to systematic observing. "Since I began observing," he explains, "I find I spend more time with children, watching how they do things. I tend to focus on two to three children a week."

Lately David has found Reggie annoying. David describes him as "hard to engage, always fidgeting, disruptive, off-task." David decided to do some focused observations of Reggie. Over the past two months, he has recorded the following observations at the end of the day.

David's Observations of Reggie

2/22: 11:00—Group time; R is able to identify only a few letters, numbers, and sounds. He fidgets, moves around the room, looks up at every noise. When he reads, he squints his eyes and turns his head to the right to get that side closer to the print. Yet he raises his hand eagerly to share information when we talk about the solar system and dinosaurs.

2/28: 2:00—Readers'/Writers' workshop: R spent 15 minutes drawing pictures of the hungry caterpillar going from branch to branch. He began fidgeting, tapping his pencil on the table, squinting when I encouraged him to try writing the words of his story.

3/19: 11:00—Large group activity: Watching Magic School Bus video. Looked at TV with head tilted to side, looking out of the corners of his eyes. Made grimacing faces. Looked at picture on TV as if he were not supposed to.

4/14: 10:30—Small group activity: Taking a walk along the nature trail to observe living things. Children called out items they found (ants, beetles etc.). R kept asking, "Where is it?" Sometimes he was somewhere else and by the time he got back, "it" was gone. When he was there, he looked all around but not at what the other children were studying. He had difficulty walking on the path, kept tripping.

4/28: 2:30—One-on-one: Letter ID Assessment: Gave R cards with letters on them to find out how many he could identify. Looked at the cards, tilted his head, squinted. Became frustrated, started saying any letter as a response.

4/30: 11:00—One-on-one: Reevaluation of Letter ID: Used large letters on 6x6 cards. R named all letters and gave sounds for most of them. Smiled proudly.

Reflection

David was struck by the pattern he saw when he read over his observations. He explains:

> I had wondered briefly if Reggie had trouble seeing, but at the same time I was involved in trying to keep him on-task. Once I reviewed my notes, I realized that my suspicion about a visual problem was probably on target. I wondered if this might be partly responsible for his distractibility, or if something else was at work here. In the midst of doing these observations, I spoke to the resource teacher, who has observed many of the same behaviors.

Next steps

David took this information to the school nurse, who contacted Reggie's mother about getting his vision evaluated. A few days ago, the school received word from the eye doctor that Reggie has a severe problem in his left eye. He now wears a patch on his right eye and will get glasses soon. David says, "I am figuring out how to support Reggie." One of the strategies David has come up with is to ask Reggie to describe what he sees before he attempts a task. For example, yesterday Reggie could not see the numbers on the left side of a game board. David and the children Reggie was playing with read the numbers to him and wrote them on large cards so he could play. David has made an appointment to talk with the nurse about her ideas and strategies; he also plans to meet with Reggie's parents. "I want to be sure Reggie is physically safe as he adjusts to the patch, and that he comes through this experience feeling good about himself."

Though David has questions about Reggie's distractibility, he has decided to focus on helping Reggie adapt to his limited vision for now. Once Reggie gets his glasses, David plans to continue observing and thinking about Reggie's sometimes limited concentration.

UNDERSTANDING DISRUPTIVE BEHAVIOR

Jolene, a teacher in an urban public school, has 29 children in her second grade classroom. An excellent classroom manager and usually quite resourceful in finding ways to support children, Jolene didn't know how to respond to Denise. She explains:

> I inherited Denise a few weeks into the school year. Other teachers warned me: "She's terrible—she's really bad." Actually, when I talk with her one-to-one, she's a pretty sweet kid. But, when I'm teaching a lesson, she doesn't seem to understand what is going on. She doesn't follow directions.

She cannot sit still or concentrate. I'm continually telling her to settle down, quit disturbing others, and stop talking.

One day, as a student teacher was conducting a whole group math lesson, Jolene stepped out of the action. In seven minutes, she observed and recorded the following running record:

JOLENE'S OBSERVATION OF DENISE

9/26: 9:00 AM —D at her desk. Lifts a pile of papers and books, searching for math book and calculator in her desk. She takes out old spelling test, stops, looks it over. Looks over at me. Gets up, walks over to me, asks me to show her the books. I do. Returns to her seat. Takes out calculator. M (child sitting next to her) takes book from absent student's desk and gives it to her.

Directions given. D looks around. Ms. P starts her off; D completes problem independently. Group discussion begins. D raises hand to answer question, calls, "Ooooo." Up on knees—looks at books of two girls across from her, lies across desk, nudges Sheryl, tells her to look at her completed page. Enters 42 on calculator, asks S, "Minus?" Starts pushing buttons before directions are given. Clears calculator. Up on knees, hand up, calls out, "50." Points to problem on the page in her book. Up on knees, looks at Ryan's book, yells, "50," writes answer in her notebook. Looks around the room. To Ryan, "Ain't we right here?" Enters 108 on calculator. Up on knees, turns around, looks at book, looks at board, talks aloud to no one in particular, smiles. Looks at other children's books. "Oh, it's 20," she says to herself. Erases the answer she has. Picks up calculator saying again, "Oh it's 20." Punches in numbers on calculator. Looks at numbers on the board, says, "Oh," and enters 584 on calculator.

Keira tells her it is the wrong number. D doesn't respond. While oral directions are given, she again punches in wrong numbers. After the numbers are written on board, she clears the calculator and enters the correct numbers. Kept looking from board to book. Looks at each number to get it entered. Says, "Man, ain't this the answer?" Rocking up on knees, leaning across the desk, asks others what to do next. Says, "804 take away," and bangs on calculator. Closes calculator and book when asked.

Reflection

Jolene saw things she wasn't able to see when she was directing the action of the class. She explains:

> I was surprised that Denise was on task so much of the time. When I'm teaching, and she's doing all that moving, my perception is that she's just fooling around. It really irks me. But after watching her, I realize her movement seems to be her way of keeping herself on task and getting the right answer. She's trying to pay attention, but she's just not really sure how to do that. She doesn't seem to understand the directions that are given orally. As I watched her I got the sense that she really wanted to do what the other children were doing, but she didn't have a clue how to proceed, unless somebody said to her, enter 50, and then pointed to the 5 and the 0.
>
> Also, I used to think she was bothering other children with all her movement and talking, but now I see it was me who was bothered. Denise wants them to help her with the answer or to know where she's supposed to be. They aren't disrupted by her at all.

Next steps

This one observation provided Jolene with several new ideas about how to support Denise. She decided to ignore some of her talking and moving. Instead of saying, "Denise are you talking again?" she now gives a silent, visual clue to help her connect to the task. For example, she might point to a number or word on a page to help her find her place and refocus on the task at hand.

Joline enlisted Denise as a partner by talking about her observations. She explained that Denise seems to have trouble understanding what to do. When Joline asked Denise if this was true, Denise said yes. Joline also said she observed that Denise was constantly moving and that she wanted to have her sit next to Shawnesse who could help her keep track of what was going on. Denise responded very positively. "She had a big smile on her face," reports Jolene.

As a result of this one observation, Jolene now has the following questions about Denise:

○ Why doesn't she understand oral directions?

○ What would help her—a peer partner? My talking more slowly? Using more visual cues?

○ What would keep her from becoming so easily frustrated?

○ Does she have a hearing or auditory processing problem? Has she ever been tested for any physical or learning problems?

Jolene will continue to observe and look for answers to these and other questions that arise.

BALANCING INDIVIDUAL AND GROUP NEEDS

Usually when we think about observing, we think of watching in order to understand individual children. But sometimes we find ourselves overfocusing on individuals and losing sight of the well-being of the larger group. As the next story illustrates, teachers sometimes have to balance the needs of individuals with the needs of the group.

Pamela, a third grade teacher, tells a story about Ben, an eight-year-old diagnosed with Attention Deficit/Hyperactivity Disorder.

Ben demanded all of my attention—or at least that was what I thought. Despite how difficult he was to manage, I was really hooked into him. He had the most wonderful smile and a great sense of humor. I sensed he was smart. When we talked one-on-one, he slowly got out his thoughts. If I was patient, he blew me away with his insights. During group time, he tried endlessly to share his ideas, but rarely could get them out.

His arrival in the classroom each day was like a tornado. He would charge through the door, bump into a cabinet or bookcase, attempt to hang his coat and backpack, but instead fling it so that it landed on the floor. Each day I'd stand by the door, ready to greet him, making what I thought were valiant efforts to calm him down and control the whirlwind of his arrival. This whirlwind behavior continued throughout the day. I made sure to be close at hand to support Ben at the beginning of each activity and transition. I guess the rest of the class figured out that Ben needed me and just sort of tolerated my attention to him. By the end of each day I was totally exhausted. I tried to talk with his mother about getting him evaluated, but she wouldn't hear of it.

Pamela explained that she documented many observations to share with his mother with the hope that eventually they would be useful if he was referred for testing. Here are a few of her notes:

PAMELA'S OBSERVATIONS OF BEN

10/14: Group time: B raises his hand flailing it wildly; I call on him. He stutters: "Em, em, I, I," shakes his head, purses his lips (seems flustered/frustrated), can't get his idea out. (Recorded after meeting: this is typical of meeting behavior)

> 10/25: 8:25 AM— Arrival: runs into the room, calls out hello. Starts for coat
> hooks, turns quickly toward cubbies, stops short, bumps into Simon.
> Simon cries out, "Watch out Ben." Ben stammers, "Sorry." Shakes his
> head. Stands still for a moment. Looks around. Rushes toward coat
> hooks. Drops backpack. Rushes over to art table with coat still on. Leans
> over to see Rachel's drawing. Takes coat off, sleeve swipes table, knocking
> Rachel's crayons to the floor. She cries out, "Ben, careful." Ben goes to
> rug and sits down, with coat still partially on.

Very often at the end of the day when Pamela would see Ronny, her principal, in the hall or the teacher's room, she needed to vent and would recount to her that day's saga of Ben. After several weeks Ronny shared her observations of Pamela with her. She observed that Pamela was stressed out, overly focused on Ben, and missing out on all the other wonderful things that were going on in her classroom. Ronny suggested to Pamela that her constant vigilance of Ben was not necessarily helping him, and that the other children were missing out on her attention. Moreover, she encouraged Pamela to observe the other children as a way to regain some of her own enthusiasm and energy about teaching. To give her a push, Ronny gave Pamela an assignment. Pamela was not to observe Ben for one week. Instead she had to come to Ronny each day with an anecdote about someone else in the class.

Reflection
Pamela explained that she was amazed at the result of Ronny's suggestions.

> At first it was a struggle for me to shift my attention away from Ben—it had become a habit for me to patrol his behavior. But I worked at it, reporting each day to Ronny about some child or an activity that had taken place. To my surprise, Ben's behavior improved somewhat as I gave him more space to figure things

out for himself. And almost as if to say that they liked having more of my attention, other kids stepped in to support Ben when necessary.

Just as Ronny had predicted, Pamela's exhaustion lessened, and her enthusiasm for her class and the work they were doing was renewed.

Next steps
By the time the week was over, Pamela had gained some perspective about Ben. She began to realize that she had taken it upon herself to manage Ben's behavior—in a sense to try to fix him—and had lost sight of the needs of the rest of the group. Although Ben's mother continued to refuse outside evaluation and intervention, Ben was making some gains in the classroom, Pamela's energy increased, and the overall dynamic of the classroom improved.

BUILDING RELATIONSHIPS WITH FAMILIES

Children benefit when the important adults in their lives work together to understand and meet their needs. In this section we see how sharing observations helps teachers and families exchange information, learn more about the children in their lives, and, over time, build partnerships to support a child's development.

Strengthening Family Ties

Leslie, a second grade teacher in a rural school, shares observations about how to strengthen the ties between a grandmother and granddaughter. She explains:

> Last year, Catherine was always in the hall for violent, aggressive behavior. Her teacher was constantly calling

her grandmother in to handle her behavior. When I scheduled my home visit this year, I decided I would try a new tack. I told her grandmother I wouldn't just call her when there was a problem. We decided I would send home a note every day.

Leslie began recording simple observations in note form. She decided to begin by recording mostly positive behaviors to show the grandmother her appreciation of Catherine and to begin building a partnership. At first she had to work hard and look carefully to find them. Over time it became easier. Here are a few examples of her observations and how she used them as notes home to Catherine's grandmother.

LESLIE'S OBSERVATIONS OF CATHERINE

9/6—During a group discussion about favorite foods, Catherine looked around and fidgeted as she waited for a turn to speak. At her turn, she said her favorite food was blueberry pancakes. She said she could eat 100 of them. She smiled when three other children agreed.

Note home: Today Catherine shared with the class how much she loves blueberry pancakes!

10/1—Catherine spent 15 minutes drawing and writing a story in her writer's journal about a dog named Henry who likes to roll in the mud and chase cats.

Note home: Today Catherine spent 15 minutes drawing and writing a story about a dog named Henry!

10/13—Catherine's face tightened when another child crumpled the edge of he painting. She moved her hands as if to pinch him. Then looked over and called me for help. I brought both children together and we talked about what had happened. Paul explained he crumpled Catherine's painting by accident when he hung his painting up on the drying line. He told Catherine he was sorry. Catherine looked at Paul and listened

---

carefully. I told her she did a good job asking for help. She smiled and said, "That's OK," to Paul.

Note home: Today Catherine did a great job solving a conflict with another child by asking for a teacher's help.

Reflection

Leslie has used her observations, not only to build her relationship with Catherine, but to strengthen Catherine's relationship with her grandmother, thus turning the grandmother into an ally in supporting Catherine—at home and in school:

Sharing these observations has had very significant impact—on Catherine, her grandmother, and on me. Catherine is starting to feel better about herself. She beamed when she told me her grandmother is proud of her. When I asked her how she knew, she said, "She hugs me a lot and hangs up the notes you send." Catherine's grandmother has called me to say how much she appreciates the positive notes. I think she is seeing Catherine in a more positive light and, hopefully, beginning to see school as her partner in helping Catherine be all she can be.

I have come to care for Catherine and the way she grabs life so fully. I asked Catherine why she was so angry last year. She told me she was frustrated. I asked her if she thought there were other things she could do that weren't violent when she got angry. She said, "I could get you." I assured Catherine that I would help her. Catherine and her grandmother have struck up a deal: If Catherine has a good year in school, her grandmother will get her a dog, something she has always wanted. I think Catherine will be a dog owner by the end of the year. I hope so.

Next steps

Leslie plans to continue observing Catherine and communicating what she sees with Catherine's grandmother. So far she has usually sent home positive observations. She wants to build on their growing sense of partnership by beginning to share with the grandmother some of Catherine's challenges in controlling her behavior. She plans to offer the grandmother ideas of things she can do at home to help Catherine learn to manage frustration and anger in socially acceptable ways.

Sharing Observations with Families

Sharon, a family child care provider, describes her experiences sharing observations with two families. She explains:

> Building good working relationships with families takes time and patience. Sometimes it is easier than others.
>
> Take the Jillsons for example. Kendra was an alert, happy, curious baby thriving in many ways. Yet her clothes were often torn and dirty and, when I changed her diaper, I often found she hadn't been cleaned well. On some cold days she arrived without a jacket—one time even without socks. And twice she came to child care so sick, I needed to send her back home. I observed and shared my observations both about Kendra's progress and delight in the world and about her physical care with her well-educated, professional, financially well-off parents. In terms of her physical care, nothing changed for the two years Kendra was in my program. I often felt angry and frustrated with her parents. Finding a colleague to express my feelings to helped me remember the most important thing was to support Kendra. I cleaned her when she was dirty and found a jacket in the lost and found for her to wear on the days when she came without one.
>
> Working with Rebecca Reilly was a different experience. I was concerned that her two-year-old Jerry's language was unclear. He was new to my program.

Sharon began observing Jerry in December. At the same time she took steps to get to know his mother and to establish a sense of trust with her. For example, she always greeted Rebecca warmly, asked how things were going, and regularly shared a story about Jerry's day. At the end of January, she arranged a conference with Jerry's mother. Here are a few examples of the observations she shared:

SHARON'S OBSERVATIONS OF JERRY

12/5—During a neighborhood walk, Jerry tugs on my sweater and talks excitedly. I'm not sure what he is saying until he gestures across the street and I see a big dog tied to a parking meter.

12/18—Jerry joins Sam and Valerie, who are constructing a road of cardboard blocks and placing rubber farm animals along it. Jerry speaks. Sam, who is almost three, looks up at him and then over to Valerie. "What's he saying?" Sam asks. Valerie looks at Jerry and Sam, and they go back to building. Jerry stands there, his eyebrows crinkle, and he kicks at their blocks. I step in.

1/6—We are making playdough. Jerry carefully pours a cup of water into the flour mixture we have made. He picks up a wooden spoon and stirs. "I do it," he says proudly looking up at me.

1/11—I asked Jerry and another child from across the room to begin putting their puzzles away. Jerry looked up, smiled, and continued working on his puzzle until he saw the other child putting hers away. He then picked up his puzzle and carried it over to the shelf.

Reflection

Sharon talks about the most effective way to share her concerns with Jerry's mother:

> I was wondering whether Jerry was having trouble hearing and thinking about how to share that possibility with his

mother. I knew it was a difficult time for her. A single mother, she had recently been let go and was just beginning a new job.

I decided to share with her many of the positive observations I had about Jerry. I then raised my concern about his hearing and language development. I began by explaining to Rebecca that I wanted Jerry to get the full benefit from being in child care. Then I said that I wanted to talk with her about something I thought was getting in the way of this goal. I shared observations of times when both the children and I had trouble understanding Jerry, and Jerry's apparent frustration in some of these situations. As Rebecca listened, her back stiffened, and I could see tears forming in her eyes. "I have to go," she told me. And she left.

Jerry's neighbor brought him and picked him up for the next three days. On the third day, I called and left a message for Rebecca, asking her to call me and reassuring her I wanted what was best for Jerry too.

She came in with him the following morning. "What should we do?" she asked.

Next steps

Sharon and Rebecca decided to continue observing in child care and at home for the next month. They set up times to talk on the phone in the evening when Jerry was in bed to exchange their observations. They agreed that if they still had concerns at the end of this time, Sharon would find out where Rebecca could take Jerry for hearing and language evaluations. And Rebecca would take him. Though Sharon wanted Jerry tested right away, she realized the month would give both her and Rebecca time to collect more information and to strengthen their partnership, which, in the long run, would benefit Jerry.

SUMMING UP

Decisions you make about the environment, daily routines, and learning opportunities in your setting affect children's learning and their sense of competence. When you observe you gain insights into children's strengths, knowledge, interests, and skills. You can make adaptations that enable children to overcome obstacles and build on what they know well. Observing can help you:

- ☼ **Individualize your program.** Observing can help you adapt the physical environment to promote exploration, interactions, and learning and to shape daily routines to give children a sense of continuity with home and the opportunity to feel a sense of mastery.

- ☼ **Individualize instruction.** Children learn best when what they are learning is meaningful. You can use what you learn about children's interests, strengths, and experiences to tailor learning opportunities.

- ☼ **Identify a health issue.** Because you spend so much time with the children, you are in the position to "catch" patterns of behavior that may indicate health problems.

- ☼ **Understand disruptive behavior.** Observing can give you insights into behavior you might otherwise find frustrating. Seeing through a child's eyes can help you be responsive and supportive.

- ☼ **Balance individual and group needs.** It can be easy to get so caught up in the needs of one child that you lose sight of the rest of the group. Making sure to observe everyone can help you maintain perspective, even when one child is particularly demanding.

- ☼ **Build relationships with families.** Children benefit when they see adults working together. Observing and exchanging observations with families can help you learn more about a child, and working together with family members keeps the child's best interests in the forefront.

We have talked extensively about the benefits of observing. In the final chapter, we turn our attention to how to start observing and make it a habit. We also provide answers to frequently asked questions.

CHAPTER 7

Getting Started: Observing Every Day

For most of us, learning something new requires lots of practice. Recall when you first learned to drive, made a new recipe, or used a particular software program for the first time. Each step was labored, you were aware of every action. But after awhile, and with practice, it became second nature. This is true of observing as well.

But how do you get started? And once you begin, how do you keep on going? This chapter begins with some tips for getting started with observing, some reasons to keep on going, and strategies to make observation part of your daily routine. In addition, we answer frequently asked questions about observing.

TIPS FOR GETTING STARTED

The caregivers and teachers we talked with confirm that once you begin observing regularly, you get hooked. However, getting started demands conscious effort. We recommend that you set up a structure that forces you to observe and record regularly and then to reflect on what you've observed.

We asked many teachers for advice on how to get started as a more purposeful observer. Here are some of their tips.

Remember, there's no time like the present

Most of us are good at coming up with excuses to keep us from tackling something new. "I can't start until I have all the class routines in order." "I'll start next month, when I have a little more time." "I'll start when my new assistant arrives." When it comes to observing, you can begin anytime. As one third grade teacher said:

> Whenever you begin, you're sure to learn something interesting.

Don't let worries about doing it right get in your way

Many teachers feel that they aren't going about observing in the right way, so they end up not observing at all. In the words of one teacher:

> I'm the type of person who wants to do it right. Since I'm not really sure what I'm supposed to do, and how I'm supposed to organize my notes, I'm too nervous—I can't seem to get started.

Observing is an ongoing learning process and, no matter how many years you spend observing children, you will refine your methods continually.

Find something interesting to watch and watch it

Some teachers find that the best way to begin is just to look around. When you find something interesting happening, stop what you are doing, take two minutes, and look and listen. Make a few notes about what you see and hear. Try this once a day for a week and see how much you learn. Or select one skill or set of related skills that you don't know very much about. Make a matrix for your class, then begin observing. You might be surprised by how much more you know than you thought you did.

Work with a colleague

Working with a partner often makes a new task more enjoyable and easier to handle. Your observing partner can be someone who works in your room, next door, or down the hall. Take turns observing. If you don't share a classroom, combine your children in one room for a story or other activity. One of you leads and the other observes a few children. Alternatively, go to your partner's room when your children are at music or art. Then switch. Talk with each other about what you saw. A second grade teacher shares her enthusiasm:

> You can't really learn to be a good observer alone. Partner up. Go to another teacher's room. Observe for her. Talk about what you saw. Let your partner come to your room and observe. You'll be so amazed at what each of you saw, how different your perceptions were. It is great to have someone to bounce ideas off of—someone to say, "Hey, I never thought about it like that."

Start small

Give yourself a manageable assignment. Decide who and what you want to observe and set a time limit. For example:

✪ Observe children in terms of a particular skill or set of skills for one week. You might want to watch and listen to how children use language, interact with peers, or use strategies to solve problems. Generate a few questions related to the skill to help you know what to watch for. If you are observing language use, for example, you might ask yourself:

   - Do the children use single words or speak in sentences?
   - Are they asking questions and, if so, what kinds?
   - Do they use language to express feelings?
   - What kind of language do they use to retell a story?

- Observe two or three children for a week. Like this infant caregiver, you might select children you don't know very well.

  I focus on observing two babies each week. It doesn't mean I don't pay attention to the others, but having "focus children" helps ensure that I don't get so caught up in daily routines I forget to observe.

- Have a conversation with a different child each day and jot down some notes either during the conversation or right after. A second grade teacher said:

  I have intentional conversations with children to gain insight about how they think. Before I was a regular observer, I didn't stop and listen carefully to what children were saying.

- Observe at the same time each day for one week. For example, if you work with babies, you might want to observe during arrival each day for a week. With older children you might decide to observe during snack, choice time, or when the children write in their journals. You might want to concentrate on a few children for the week, a different child each day, or whomever catches your interest at the time.

Acknowledge and appreciate how much you can learn from observing
When you finish an observation, or at the end of week, review your notes. Ask yourself, "What did I learn?" Chances are there will be some surprises. As a toddler teacher discovered:

Observing is a bit like exercise. Everyone knows they should do it. The challenge is getting to the gym and starting. With exercise, once you see yourself gaining strength or losing weight, you're hooked!

Take a moment to think about what you have learned

When you finish an observation, or at the end of the week, review your notes. Ask yourself, "What did I learn, and how can I apply it?" As a teacher of toddlers discovered:

> You'll learn about kids and yourself in leaps and bounds. With observing, you uncover a gold mine of information. The thought and time you devote to observing is much smaller than the rewards you will reap.

REFLECT ON THE REWARDS OF OBSERVING

When you try something new, it is a good idea to reflect on how it affects you. In talking with teachers, we discovered that in addition to providing helpful information about children, the act of observing has a powerful impact on the culture of the program—the individuals and the climate. Here are some stories about how spending time tuning in to individual children changed the climate of the program and teachers' perceptions of their roles.

A teacher of toddlers shared:

> As our staff has become better observers, our program has changed. We support one another more so that each of us can have more one-on-one time observing and interacting with the children. One-on-one time is really the way to go—I know I feel better about myself when I'm doing more responsive caregiving.

Teachers of older children described how the children became more accepting of their one-on-one time with others, once they understood what the teacher was doing when she was observing, and that they too would get a turn for undivided attention. A first grade teacher noted:

> I think the culture in my room is very different now from before. For one, kids know from experience that I take the time to talk

with them and really listen. They look forward to their conversations with me—if they don't get to show me their work today, they know they'll get a chance tomorrow.

A veteran second grade teacher talked about how she came to see her role differently. As she stepped back, the children relied more on each other and used each other as resources:

I've been teaching for 20 years. Until recently I was pretty traditional—lots of whole group instruction. As I've gotten more into observing, I structure many more small group activities. This gives me much more one-on-one time with children. They rely more on each other now than they used to—before I was always the one they came to.

Teachers shared stories about how their actions as observers increased children's motivation and pride in their work. This teacher discovered that her recording strategy, devised to help her remember to observe, had the added benefit of increasing children's competence:

I keep a sheet of paper for each child on the front wall under the chalkboard. When I see a child do or say something I want to remember, I jot it down on a sticky and put it on that child's sheet. I started this system to make sure I was observing everyone. It has turned into a means of showing children my respect. They frequently ask me to write things down and call me to come and see specific things they are doing. They take great pride in the fact that I notice and care enough to write notes about them.

A preschool teacher told a story about how interested her children were in what she was writing:

At first I felt that I shouldn't let the children know what I was doing. I kept trying to observe and record by sneaking around. Then one day a child said, "Hey—what are you writing?" I told him that I was writing down things I observed. With a big grin he said, "Write something down about me." I guess I was slow to see the advantages of letting the children know. For one, the children get so excited about showing me what they are doing. When they see the teacher write down what they are doing—it must be significant—it gives more importance to their work. I also think that my writing observations models literacy for them.

A kindergarten teacher told us how observing made him appreciate how much children know. For him, learning to listen to children resulted in children becoming more independent and confident:

I really learn interesting things about kids by listening to them, especially when I eavesdrop on the conversations they have with each other. I'm constantly amazed by how much children learn from one another—in fact, how much they actually know about things I didn't know they know. This is a new realization for me, something I didn't really value before. I think they've picked up on it. As I spend more time showing respect for children's knowledge by stepping back and listening, they spend more time exchanging information and ideas with one another.

We encourage you to take some time for reflection. As you begin observing, or continue to observe, think about how what you are doing affects you, the children, and your program.

A second grade teacher sums it up:

Once you see its value, it is hard to stop observing.

MAKE OBSERVING PART OF YOUR DAILY ROUTINE

Over time, observing and recording will become more natural, and the formal structures you've used to get started will lessen in importance. As a first grade teacher said:

Once you get into a routine and rhythm, you've got it.

The caregivers and teachers we have talked with confirm that, once you begin observing, you get hooked. But to make observing a habit, you have to make it fit your daily routine. As one infant caregiver put it:

> I want to get to where observing is like a healthy lifestyle, not a diet I struggle to follow.

To incorporate observing into your schedule, set aside time for observing, recording, and reflecting just as you plan for the other activities and routines of the day and week. Here are some ideas caregivers and teachers have shared.

☼ Identify one or two times during the day or week when you can easily step out of the action and watch what children are doing. Write the word "OBSERVING" right into your schedule so that you remember to do it. Here's what one toddler caregiver said about this:

> I have to set up observation like any daily routine. I put it in my schedule: Wednesdays 10:00–10:15 Observing. When you spend eight hours a day for five days each week with children, you can find ten minutes to observe.

☼ If you work with preschool or school-age children, plan some time each day when they can work or play independently or in small groups. This will allow you to step out of the action and observe for a few minutes.

☼ Select an activity each day during which you know you can observe and record in the midst of the action. Some teachers decide in advance who they will observe, while others wait to see who catches their eye.

☼ Review a checklist biweekly or monthly to see what you already know and what you need to learn about individual children. Review your schedule for the week to determine when you might be able to find the information you are looking for. Note the times and what you want to focus on in your weekly plans. For example, in reviewing her checklist, a third grade teacher notices that she needs information about Joanna's scientific thinking skills. She sees that a science activity is planned for Thursday morning and notes in her plans to observe Joanna during that time.

✿ Take time to reflect on what you have observed. You may want to take a few minutes to jot notes at the end of each day.

FREQUENTLY ASKED QUESTIONS

In our conversations with caregivers and teachers across the country, many questions arise as teachers begin to observe regularly. Sometimes these questions get in the way of observing even as teachers acknowledge the importance of observing.

In some cases the answer to a question requires a change in attitude about observing; in others, there are concrete suggestions to try. Sometimes a combination of the two is required. We hope you find some of these ideas applicable to your situation—and that they inspire you to come up with your own solutions to questions and challenges you encounter.

Q: Am I doing this right?

Many teachers let their fear of observing stop them from observing at all. And as the days, weeks, and even months pass without recording one observation, any inclination to begin observing is stifled by their feeling that they have missed so much, they will never be able to catch up. As one teacher told us:

> I don't observe because I'm not sure I'm doing it right. Then, when I think I might give it a try, I feel I am so far behind, I'll never be able to learn all I should about the kids in my room. So I don't observe—and I feel bad about it.

A: Observing is a skill that takes time to master. Even the best observers find they become better observers with practice. Asking yourself, "How can I improve my observation skills?" is much more helpful than worrying whether you are doing it right. Of course, there will be times you miss something important about a child. But what you miss pales in comparison to how much you can see if you observe regularly.

Sometimes, when we begin something new, we set unrealistic expectations for ourselves. Instead of saying, "I'd like to observe in my classroom more," most of us decide we're going to observe every day. Many add that their observations will include at least three observations of activities and three observations of children. The problem with setting such high expectations is that most often, after less than a week, we feel we've failed.

Give yourself time to integrate observing into your daily schedule. Try not to set yourself up to fail by setting unrealistic goals for how much time you'll spend observing or how many notes or matrices you'll have by the end of the week.

Allow yourself time to get comfortable with your style as an observer. Give yourself a chance to experiment with methods of recording and realize that trial and error is often the route to success.

Q: It is hard for me to step out of the action because I would rather be doing than watching. How can I develop the habit of observing regularly?

Have you ever felt this way? For many caregivers and teachers, "doing" comes naturally. The give-and-take of interacting with children is immediately rewarding. And, as you know only too well, there is always a child who needs extra attention or something else to attend to.

Some caregivers and teachers feel guilty about taking time to step back to observe. They are afraid they are not doing their job unless they are interacting directly with children. This myth is reinforced when their co-workers and supervisors who do not value observation send them withering glances.

Still others are afraid of "losing control" if they step back. They fear children may "act out," or that they may lose the feel of what is going on if they are not directly involved.

A: As we discussed in Chapter 4, you have options. You can observe by participating in the action and by reflecting on the action after the fact.

In a situation where you want or feel you need to step back, the decision whether to do so often boils down to two things: how you see your role and your view of observing. If you feel you are the center of everything that is going on, it is little wonder that you find it difficult to step back. On the other hand, if you see yourself as a facilitator of learning and feel that children learn from interacting with their environment, each other, other adults who may be present, and you, it is easier to believe that positive things can happen even if you are not actively involved.

And what about your view of observing? How important is it to doing your job well? As you know by now, we believe that observing is essential to teaching and assessing young children. Although situations will come up that need your immediate hands-on attention, observing is as valuable as anything else you do during the day. It can be difficult to continue observing when a co-worker doesn't feel the same way—and even more of a challenge when a supervisor feels observing is a waste of time. Unfortunately, there is no easy way to turn someone into an observer. It is a process that often takes time. You may want to explain, "I observe in order to be able to get to know children and respond to their individual needs." It may help to share with them concrete examples of how observing has guided your response to a child. You may also want to share this page—or this entire book. In the meantime, we encourage you to stand firm and continue observing.

Here are a few suggestions to help you make "stepping out of the action" more successful:

- ✿ Remember, you can see a lot in a short amount of time.

- ✿ Discuss how to handle observing with your co-worker(s) (if you have any) beforehand. Cue your co-worker when you are ready to "step out" so the co-worker will know to focus on the whole group.

- ✿ Arrange for an extra pair of hands if there is a child or situation that will require some intense observing.

- ✿ Choose times to step back when most children are engaged.

- ✿ Let children know what you are doing and encourage them to get help from one another.

Q: I'm too busy to observe. How can I find the time?

It can be a challenge to find time to go to the bathroom or eat lunch some days, let alone observe, even under the best of conditions. And when your class size is larger than optimum, the demands on your time are greater still. As one caregiver put it:

If the day is crazy, you can't observe—even if you have questions.

A: There will always be difficult days. But does that mean you are not observing? Or that you may not have time to record what you see, or even think about it until things quiet down?

Because observing is a way of being with children, you observe no matter what is going on around you. If you are having trouble recording observations, ask for help. If you provide them with an easy-to-use framework, supervisors, colleagues, student teachers, and special area teachers can, for example, jot down a child's language or check off whether a child completed a puzzle. Don't let your concern that someone may end up recording observations that aren't objective or accurate prevent you from enlisting help. Remember, you can decide which notes to keep and use.

Ironically, if you are having too many crazy days, observing more often may help you identify the cause of the craziness—and give you insight about ways to regain a sense of order.

Q: How can I get my children to let me observe?

Sometimes teachers tell us that they want to observe, they have their tools ready, they start observing, and then they're interrupted by numerous requests from their students. Balancing the ongoing needs of children and your need to observe and record is a skill that requires some practice and advance planning.

A: In trying to balance meeting many needs with observing, here are several ideas that may help. Some of these apply to children of all ages; others are for a particular age group.

- ☼ **Some situations require an immediate response.** There will be many situations in which responding to children directly is more important than recording notes that can be jotted down later. Chances are, the younger the children you work with, the more often you will end up putting aside your notes. That's okay. It's the way it should be to keep children safe and show them they can trust you.

    With infants and toddlers, a prompt response is often essential. If you are jotting down a note about Jason, and you spot Rachita climbing on the back of the sofa across the room, your priority is to move quickly to protect her from falling. Your notes can wait.

- ☼ **Work closely with your co-workers.** Learn to cue each other using a few words, a look, or a gesture. When a co-worker catches your eye and knows, for example, that you are going to step out of the action for a few minutes to jot down some notes, she realizes that she will have to keep her eyes on the whole group—and alert you if she needs you. If you are the sole adult in a family child care home, consider asking a parent to come occasionally so you have the opportunity to step back.

○ **Talk with children about what you are doing.** As children get older, you can explain what "observing" is— how you watch and listen to them to get to know them better. Some teachers bring this up at a class meeting by asking children, "How do you think I learn about what you do and know?" To make the point more concrete, you may want to ask children to tell you something they would like you to watch. Then, after you have observed, talk together about what you learned. Often we forget how little time it takes to give children explanations about what we're doing. Sometimes, a simple, "I'm busy observing now, I'll come and talk to you in a few minutes," is all that's required.

○ **Arrange the environment to increase children's independence.** Creating a safe environment is the first priority so that children can be free to explore and play, and you can be free from worrying about hazards, such as electric outlets without covers and fish tanks that can be toppled by jostling of enthusiastic "fish feeders." Diaper changing can be a time for enjoying being together when supplies are organized and easily accessible. Older toddlers can wash their own hands when they use the stepstool you've placed near the sink, and preschoolers can put their toys away more independently if the shelves are labeled with pictures showing where things go.

✿ **Teach children ways to function more independently.**
Teaching classroom procedures and routines (how to
wash and dry hands, the rules about getting a drink of
water, etc.) can save time. In addition, you can teach
children strategies to try to solve their own problems
before approaching you for help. Teachers use many
different strategies to increase their students'
self-reliance. In classrooms that use the "three before
me" rule, for example, students try to get their problem
solved by asking three other people for help before
asking the teacher. These and other strategies make a
noticeable difference in the amount of time teachers
have to observe. When teachers begin to encourage
independence, they are often amazed by how much
children can do by themselves.

**Q: How can I find time to write everything down—let alone
review what I have recorded?**

Not having enough time comes up in every workshop we have
given about observing. We hope two of the messages you take
away from this book are: you can and do observe without
recording, and recording is valuable because it gives you
something to refer to later on. As one teacher told us:

> Recording takes away the pressure of trying to remember
> thousands of details. It also keeps them from getting all mixed
> up inside your head.

A: Once again, be realistic. Don't try to write everything down—
especially at the beginning of the year as you are getting to know
families, establishing routines, and getting into sync with your
co-workers. We recommend you focus on being there—on
observing the special details that make each child unique and
building relationships. Remember, it is unnecessary and unrealistic
to think about recording something about every child or every event
in the day.

As things begin to settle down, put observing and recording into your daily schedule two or three times a week. To help you find time to jot down notes during busy times, think ahead a bit when things are calm. Be clear about what you want to look for. Consider times of the day that lend themselves more easily to observing such as small-group time and when children are playing independently. Record a word or two, a sentence, marks, or other symbols that have meaning to you on a checklist or grid.

Take the same approach to finding time to read and think about what you have recorded. You may find that a structured plan will help make reflecting on your written observations a natural part of your work. One teacher told us she set a timer for 10 minutes every Tuesday afternoon to read her notes.

> Even though I couldn't read every observation in that amount of time, I was reading more than I had been: nothing. Slowly it got to be a habit.

Q: How can I be objective when I care so much and am so involved in the lives of these children?

Children need you to care. At the same time, they need your objectivity, something that is difficult for their families to give them. You need your objectivity to see and respond to children for who they are. Giving both your care and your objectivity requires an ongoing balancing act, which is at the core of being a professional who works with young children and families.

A: You are your own best resource in your work with children. The fact that you worry about your ability to remain impartial can give you confidence. Recognizing that you may not be objective is the first step toward becoming an effective observer. This, in turn, will help you get to know children and make decisions that best support their development and learning.

We encourage you to reread Chapter 3 in which we take a look at who you are as an observer and what you bring to observing. Also, ask a colleague to come observe with you when you are concerned that your feelings might be getting in the way of seeing a child clearly. Having outside observations to compare with yours will help you gauge your objectivity and take a caring step back if necessary.

CLOSING THOUGHTS

It's very easy to get caught up in the "how-tos" of observing and lose sight of its power to make a difference in your work with children. "Should I record my observations on index cards or large stickies?" "Should I observe only during choice time?" "Should I record running records or use a rating scale?"

It isn't that the specifics don't matter—they do—but only as a means to the end—a means to getting to know, respect, and appreciate children and to intervene in ways that enable them to be successful learners. Otherwise we just end up with a stack of notes crumpled up in the back of a drawer.

As we've discussed in this book, observing is an attitude of openness, necessary for good teaching. We hope we have convinced you to become aware of yourself as an observer and to take full advantage of the rich insights observing offers you every day. Watching, listening, reflecting, and relating are as important as anything else you do during the day. The children and their families will benefit. And so will you.

Observing can make teaching more personally and intellectually satisfying. There's nothing more rewarding than coming to understand and appreciate a child whom you didn't really like or found puzzling. Without observing, Amy would have continued to see Johnny as chaotic, Margo's picture of Tony would have been limited by what others had said, and Judy would have not been able to get past her feelings to discover Rachel's enthusiasm and sense of humor.

It is energizing to learn and to succeed in making a connection with a child or family that seemed outside your reach. As an engaged learner, you will imbue your setting with a sense of the importance and rewards of being open to learning. Your curiosity, questioning, and reflecting will lead you to new insights and to modeling learning and growing for the children and families in your group. Yours will truly be an environment where the young— and not so young—are encouraged to explore and discover.

As we have said before, the key to your success as an observer is making observation work for you. While there are guidelines to follow, the decisions you make every day as you begin to observe regularly must take into account your preferences and needs. It won't always be easy. You are sure to come up against obstacles sooner or later. But we guarantee, if you make a commitment to observe children regularly, your teaching will become more interesting, rewarding, and effective.

Resources

This resource list is by no means comprehensive, but it does include those resources that have been especially helpful to us in our work as teachers and staff developers.

Almy, Millie, and Celia Genishi. *Ways of Studying Children,* Revised Edition. New York: Teachers College Press, 1979.

This book provides an in-depth examination of how to use observation to study children—how they think and learn. It is appropriate for teachers working with children from preschool through the primary grades.

Beaty, Janice, J. *Observing Development of the Young Child (3rd ed.).* New York: Macmillan Publishing Company, 1994.

Beaty focuses on observation of the preschool child. She includes extensive information about child development, strategies for observing and documenting learning, and suggestions for interventions.

Bickart, Toni S., Judy R. Jablon, and Diane Trister Dodge. *Building the Primary Classroom: A Complete Guide to Teaching and Learning.* Washington, DC: Teaching Strategies, Inc. and Portsmouth, NH: Heinemann, 1999.

This comprehensive book provides teachers with specific strategies for supporting children's learning in the primary grades. Part I describes six strategies for building the primary classroom; Part II outlines what children should be learning in each curriculum area and how to shape instruction by applying the six strategies.

Cohen, Dorothy, Virginia Stern, and Nancy Balaban. *Observing and Recording the Behavior of Young Children (4th ed.).* New York: Teachers College Press, 1997.

This is an excellent resource for a more detailed discussion of observation and recording infant, toddler, and preschool children's behavior. The book includes extensive information about child development and the methods and tools for documenting observations.

Colker, Laura J. *Observing Young Children: Learning to Look, Looking to Learn.* Washington, DC: Teaching Strategies, Inc., 1995.

The video and accompanying Trainer's Guide helps early childhood educators use observations to learn about children and individualize their programs, evaluate their programs so they can make necessary adjustments to the environment and/or curriculum, and measure children's progress and acquisition of skills.

Dichtelmiller, Margo L., Judy R. Jablon, Aviva B. Dorfman, Dorothea B. Marsden, and Samuel J. Meisels. *Work Sampling in the Classroom: A Teacher's Manual.* Ann Arbor, MI: Rebus, Inc., 1997.

Work Sampling in the Classroom describes how to use a systematic approach to performance assessment. Specifically, it provides many suggestions about observation.

Dodge, Diane Trister, and Laura J. Colker. *The Creative Curriculum® for Early Childhood, Third Edition.* Washington, DC: Teaching Strategies, Inc., 1992.

This child development-based curriculum shows teachers how to create an effective learning environment for preschool and kindergarten children. The Child Development and Learning Checklist offers a practical way for teachers to observe and document children's progress.

Dombro, Amy Laura, Laura J. Colker, and Diane Trister Dodge. *The Creative Curriculum® for Infants & Toddlers, Revised Edition.* Washington, DC: Teaching Strategies, Inc., 1999.

This curriculum provides a comprehensive, yet easy-to-use framework for planning and implementing a quality program for children under three and their families. Throughout are examples showing how caregivers and teachers use information gathered through observation to create responsive relationships with children and families.

Drummond, Mary Jane. *Learning to See: Assessment through Observation.* York, ME: Stenhouse Publishers, 1994.

In *Learning to See*, Drummond examines observation in relation to instruction, emphasizing the importance of using what is learned from observation to modify instruction. The focus of the book is preschool and elementary-age children.

Helm, Judy, H., Sallee Beneke, and Kathy Steinheimer. *Windows on Learning: Documenting Young Children's Work.* New York: Teachers College Press, 1998.

Windows on Learning presents a comprehensive approach to documenting young children's learning that describes how to collect, organize, and share information, and how to use insights from the documentation process to inform curriculum and instruction. It combines theory, practical tips, and stories to highlight the importance of observation.

Jablon, Judy R., Dorothea B. Marsden, Samuel J. Meisels, and Margo L. Dichtelmiller. *The Work Sampling System Omnibus Guidelines, Third Edition. Volume I.* Ann Arbor, MI: Rebus Inc., 1994.

This volume outlines developmental expectations in all domains for children age 3 through third grade. It is one component of *The Work Sampling System*, a comprehensive approach to instructional performance assessment.

Katz, Lilian, and Diane McClellan. *Fostering Children's Social Competence: The Teacher's Role.* Washington, DC: NAEYC, 1997.

Katz and McClellan discuss principles and strategies teachers can use to support the development of children's social skills. Included in this book is a discussion of the importance of teachers' relationships with children in promoting their success. This is an excellent resource for preschool and elementary teachers.

Judy Jablon, M.S., is an early childhood curriculum and assessment specialist. After twelve years as a classroom teacher working with primary grade children, she extended her work in the field to include college teaching, staff development, and writing. She is an author of *What Every Parent Needs to Know About 1st, 2nd & 3rd Grades, Building the Primary Classroom,* and a developer of *The Work Sampling System.*

Ms. Jablon has served as consultant on numerous staff development initiatives with schools, districts, and state departments of education implementing the Work Sampling System. She designed a staff development program on observing young children for Head Start and preschool teachers and assistants in the Montgomery County Public School District in Maryland. She is currently consulting with the Maryland State Department of Education to design and implement the Maryland Model for School Readiness, a comprehensive staff development initiative for preschool and kindergarten teachers.

Amy Laura Dombro, M.S. is the author of numerous articles and books on infants and toddlers and family child care, including *The Creative Curriculum® for Infants & Toddlers.* She has extensive experience training Head Start and child care staff, and consults for national organizations in the areas of child care and community mobilization.

Ms. Dombro was a member of the Advisory Committee on Services for Families with Infants and Toddlers that guided the design of the new Early Head Start program. She began her professional career by serving for eight years as the director of Bank Street College's Infant and Family Center in New York City.

Margo L. Dichtelmiller, Ph.D., is an Assistant Professor in Early Childhood Education at Eastern Michigan University. In addition to her teaching, she consults with early childhood programs, providing staff development on assessment, curriculum, and program evaluation. She is a developer of *The Work Sampling System*, and has consulted with the St. Paul Public Schools and the State of Minnesota in their implementation of Work Sampling. She currently provides training on observation and child development to Head Start programs and Early Head Start programs on issues related to observation and child development.

Dr. Dichtelmiller received her Ph.D. from the University of Michigan, where she coordinated a longitudinal study of high risk infants. Prior to her doctoral work, Dr. Dichtelmiller taught infants and preschool children with special needs in home and classroom-based settings for nine years.

Resources for Parents

A Parent's Guide to Infant/Toddler Programs
Promotes a partnership with parents by explaining how responsive care fosters the development of young children. #CB0033, **$22.50** (set of 10)
Also available in Spanish: #CB0034, **$22.50** (set of 10)

A Parent's Guide to Early Childhood Education
Explains what happens in a developmentally appropriate early childhood program and the important role parents play in helping their children succeed in school and in life.
#CB0075, **$22.50** (set of 10) (English edition)
#CB0089, **$22.50** (set of 10) (Spanish edition)
#CB0060, **$22.50** (set of 10) (Chinese edition)

Preschool for Parents
Shows how high-quality preschools
use knowledge of child development
to plan rich and varied play experiences
that enhance emotional intelligence, social
skills, and school readiness.
#CB0009, **$12.95**

What Every Parent Needs to Know About 1st, 2nd, & 3rd Grades
An invaluable tool to help parents
understand best practice in the primary grades.
#CB0061, **$12.95**

VIDEOS

The Creative Curriculum®: A 37-minute, award-winning videotape that shows how children learn in each interest area.
#CB0072, **$99.50**. Also available with Spanish subtitles: #CB0014, **$99.50**

Observing Young Children: Learning to Look, Looking to Learn: This 30-minute videotape illustrates how staff can use ongoing observation to learn about each child, measure children's progress, and evaluate their program. #CB0054, **$55.00**

Order online at our Web site, www.TeachingStrategies.com, or call (800) 637-3652